SPECULUM ANNIVERSARY MONOGRAPHS

FIVE

SPIRITUALITY AND ADMINISTRATION

SPECULUM ANNIVERSARY MONOGRAPHS

FIVE

Spirituality and Administration

The Role of the Bishop in Twelfth-Century Auxerre

CONSTANCE BRITTAIN BOUCHARD

THE MEDIAEVAL ACADEMY OF AMERICA   1979

The publication of this book was made possible by funds contributed
to the Mediaeval Academy during the Semi-Centennial Fund Drive.

Contents

Figures

ABBREVIATIONS

AASS	*Acta sanctorum quotquot toto orbe coluntur*
Arch. Nat.	Paris, Archives Nationales
Arch. Yonne	Auxerre, Archives départementales de l'Yonne
Bibl. Auxerre	Auxerre, Bibliothèque municipale d'Auxerre
Gallia Christiana	*Gallia Christiana in provincias ecclesiasticas distributa*
Gesta	*Gesta pontificum Autissiodorensium*, ed. L.-M. Duru, *Bibliothèque historique de l'Yonne*, 1 (Auxerre, 1850), 309–509. Cited by page number.
Hefele-Leclercq, *Histoire des conciles*	Charles-Joseph Hefele, *Histoire des conciles*, trans. and aug. H. Leclercq, 10 vols. (Paris, 1907–38). Cited by volume and page number.
Mansi	J. D. Mansi, ed., *Sacrorum conciliorum nova et amplissima collecta*
MGH SS	*Monumenta Germaniae Historica, Scriptores*
PL	J. P. Migne, ed., *Patrologiae cursus completus, Series Latina*
Quantin, 1, 2, 3	Maximilien Quantin, ed., *Cartulaire général de l'Yonne*, 2 vols. (Auxerre, 1854–60); *Recueil de pièces pour faire suite au Cartulaire général de l'Yonne* (Auxerre, 1873). Cited by volume and document number, followed by the page number.
RHGF	*Recueil des historiens des Gaules et de la France*
Robert of St.-Marien	Robert of St.-Marien, *Chronicon*, ed. O. Holder-Egger, MGH SS 26:219–87. Cited by page number.
RS	*Rerum Brittanicarum medii aevi scriptores* (Rolls Series)

INTRODUCTION

The bishop played a central role in the religious life of the twelfth century. He was the spiritual leader and chief executive of the churches in his diocese and one of the major landowners of the region. Contemporary ecclesiastics, especially the cathedral canons who elected the bishop at this time, expected a good bishop to present an example of the spiritual life and to be an effective administrator, both of diocesan affairs and of the episcopate's temporal possessions. The bishop's role did not remain constant throughout the twelfth century—there were changes in the contemporary definition of spirituality and of administrative duties, and changes in the way the men in office carried out their obligations.

To explore the nature and evolution of the bishop's role in this period, I have taken the example of one diocese, the see of Auxerre in northern Burgundy. The twelfth-century sources for the history of the diocese of Auxerre are unusually rich. Particularly important is the series of episcopal biographies, all of them written by canons of the cathedral who, with one exception, knew their subjects personally. Fuller than those produced at any other French see of this time, the biographies are quite detailed (they average some 3,000 words; the longest is about 10,000 words). The series has never been thoroughly studied. It presents a valuable picture of the bishops of Auxerre, a picture which is supplemented by the many surviving episcopal charters.

The role of the medieval bishop has not before been examined using the evidence of episcopal biographies. Historians of canon law have studied contemporary ideas on the nature of the episcopal office by way of the legal and political structure surrounding the bishop. Robert Benson, for example, treated the process by which an elected bishop assumed his duties as a key to understanding medieval views of episcopal powers and responsibilities.[1] But this approach does not exhaust the possibilities for investigation of the bishop's role. (Auxerre, like most sees, produced no surviving twelfth-century materials analyzing abstract legal principles on the theoretical level, as distinct from binding legal arguments.) Much can be learned about the nature of the episcopal office from biographies and charters.

1. Robert L. Benson, *The Bishop-Elect* (Princeton, 1968), p. vii.

1

Biographies can be used to reveal changes taking place in the concept of the office, even when the structure of the office was not changing; archival documents issued by the bishops may suggest the bishops' own priorities. Using these sources I have attempted to analyze the changes that occurred in the role of the bishop in twelfth-century Auxerre. The progressive changes in the activities of the bishops will be correlated with changes in contemporary concepts, as expressed in the biographies, of what a bishop ought to do.

The Twelfth-Century Bishops of Auxerre

For the purpose of this essay I consider the twelfth century to have lasted from 1092 to 1220, during which period there were seven bishops in the diocese of Auxerre.[2]

Humbaud, 1092–1114
Hugh of Montaigu, 1115–1136
Hugh of Mâcon, 1136–1151
Alain, 1152–1167
William of Toucy, 1167–1181
Hugh of Noyers, 1183–1206
William of Seignelay, 1207–1220

The limits of 1092 and 1220 have been chosen both because they mark the boundaries of a period in the history of the diocese in which the bishop was its chief authority and because the quality and accessibility of the sources is better for these seven bishops than for those preceding or succeeding them. These 130 years in the ecclesiastical history of Auxerre span the period from the end of the domination of the bishopric by the local secular powers to the rise of major influence by the king and the pope: Humbaud's immediate predecessor was the son of the local count, who himself had succeeded the son of the local viscount; William of Seignelay, who had been exiled by the king for a brief period during his pontificate, was translated in 1220, against his will and on the direct order of the pope, to the see of Paris. The 130 years in which the bishops of Auxerre directed the spiritual and temporal life of their diocese, more or less without such domination by count, king, or pope, are recorded in biographies longer and more detailed than those from either the eleventh or the thirteenth century.

2. Slightly different dates for some of these bishops are given by Ulysse Chevalier, Pius Bonifacius Gams, L.-M. Duru, and Auguste Longnon. None of these entirely agree with each other, though the differences are not large. I have established the dates of the various episcopates for myself, using both the references in the contemporary biographies to the length of time a man held the see and all available dated documents.

Most of the seven twelfth-century bishops of Auxerre were local and noble in origin. Four had lived all their lives in the Auxerrois: Humbaud, William of Toucy, Hugh of Noyers, and William of Seignelay. These same four all came from the secular clergy, having served as dignitaries in the cathedral chapters at Auxerre or Sens, or even at both, before their elections. The other three, all abbots before their elections, had passed their childhoods in regions outside the Auxerrois. Two of them, Hugh of Montaigu and Hugh of Mâcon, were nevertheless abbots of local monasteries, respectively St.-Germain (for fifteen years) and Pontigny (for twenty-two years). The only stranger to the region was Alain, a native of Flanders who was abbot of Larrivour, near Troyes, at the time of his election. Alain was the only one of the seven not elected by the Auxerre cathedral chapter; after an irreconcilable split in the chapter, he was designated as bishop by Bernard of Clairvaux and Eugenius III. He was the only bishop of the seven who abdicated. In addition, Alain was the only twelfth-century bishop not known to be from a noble family; perhaps those in Auxerre who recorded his life were simply ignorant of his family because he was not from Burgundy, but there is no necessary reason to assume that he was of noble origin.

All of these bishops except Alain are known to have had relatives in positions of importance in local or nearby churches. Humbaud made his nephew Ulger provost of the cathedral chapter while he was bishop. Hugh of Montaigu, who had started his ecclesiastical career at Cluny before becoming abbot of St.-Germain in 1100, was nephew of Hugh, abbot of Cluny (1049–1109), and first cousin of Rainald, abbot of Vézelay (1106–1125), and of Gervais, his successor as abbot of St.-Germain in 1115. Hugh of Mâcon made two of his nephews canons in the cathedral chapter of Auxerre; his nephew Stephen, whom he had made provost, unsuccessfully tried to have himself elected bishop to succeed his uncle. William of Toucy was younger brother of Hugh, archbishop of Sens (1143–1168), under whom he had served as archdeacon before his election to Auxerre. He was succeeded by Hugh of Noyers, his distant cousin, who was nephew of Gui, archbishop of Sens (1176–1193), and Agnes, abbess of St.-Julien of Auxerre (1144–1174). Hugh was succeeded in turn by his cousin William of Seignelay, also nephew of Archbishop Gui and Abbess Agnes, and brother of Manasses, bishop of Orléans.

The origins of the men who became bishop of Auxerre in the twelfth century are typical of the origins of most contemporary bishops of northern France.[3] The surveys carried out by the Institut de Droit Canonique de

3. Constance B. Bouchard, "The Geographical, Social and Ecclesiastical Origins of the

Strasbourg found that the majority of bishops studied came originally from the region of their diocese if not the diocese itself, that roughly half of the bishops definitely came from the nobility (the actual figure may well be higher, as the family origins are not known for all bishops), and that it was not uncommon for a see to be headed by a series of relatives or for relatives simultaneously to hold adjacent sees.[4] In the contemporary Rhineland an even higher proportion of the bishops can be demonstrated to have been noble than is the case for France.[5] Auxerre is typical of many French sees in that several bishops in the first half of the century came from the regular clergy, but their successors in the second half of the century came more and more from the secular clergy.[6] These seven bishops also experienced a stability common in twelfth-century France: five of the seven died in office, and they averaged more than seventeen years each as bishop, an average somewhat higher than that of most contemporary French sees, although in England the average length of time a bishop held his see was as long as twenty-eight years in the middle of the twelfth century.[7]

The Bishopric of Auxerre

The twelfth-century city of Auxerre was dominated, as it still is today, by the cathedral of St.-Etienne, rising from the top of a hill above the surrounding town. Auxerre had been the center of a diocese for some 800 years at the beginning of the twelfth century, and the bishops had had their church on the highest point of the city for over 600 years. The cathedral,

---

Bishops of Auxerre and Sens in the Central Middle Ages," *Church History* 46 (1977), 281-84. There has been new interest among scholars in episcopal origins in recent years; besides the works cited in this article and below, see, most recently, the articles on German and Italian episcopal origins in *Le istituzioni ecclesiastiche della "Societas Christiana" dei secoli XI-XII: Diocesi, pievi e parrocchie*, Miscellanea del Centro di studi medioevali 8 (Milan, 1977).

4. Jean Gaudemet, "Recherches sur l'épiscopat médiéval en France," in *Proceedings of the Second International Congress of Medieval Canon Law*, ed. Stephan Kuttner and J. Joseph Ryan (Vatican City, 1965), pp. 139-50. See also Bernard Guillemain, "Les origines des évêques en France aux XIe et XIIe siècles," *Le istituzioni ecclesiastiche della "Societas Christiana" dei secoli XI-XII: Papato, cardinalato ed episcopato*, Miscellanea del Centro di studi medioevali 7 (Milan, 1974), pp. 381-83.

5. Aloys Schulte, *Der Adel und die deutsche Kirche im Mittelalter* (Stuttgart, 1910), pp. 61-73. For a recent confirmation of Schulte's findings, see Carlrichard Brühl, "Die Sozialstruktur des deutschen Episkopats im 11. und 12. Jahrhundert," *Le istituzioni ecclesiastiche* [1977], p. 48.

6. Marcel Pacaut, *Louis VII et les élections épiscopales dans le royaume de France* (Paris, 1957), p. 115. Guillemain, "Les origines des évêques," p. 386.

7. David Knowles, *The Episcopal Colleagues of Archbishop Thomas Becket* (Cambridge, 1951), p. 6.

with the episcopal palace and the houses of the canons, was protected by the old Gallo-Roman city walls (see Figure 1). Within the walls and only a few yards from the cathedral edifice was the chapel of Notre-Dame-la-Cité, subject to the cathedral chapter. During the second half of the twelfth century new walls were built by the local counts to encompass the town that had grown up on the west bank of the Yonne around the cathedral, including a number of churches that had existed outside the walls since the early Middle Ages: St.-Germain, a house of Benedictine monks dating from the sixth century, which had faced the cathedral across a narrow swampy valley from behind its own walls; and the churches of St.-Pèlerin, St.-Pierre, Notre-Dame-la-Dehors, and St.-Eusèbe, all of which became priories of canons regular during the twelfth century. Across the river from the walled city stood the old churches of St.-Martin and St.-Marien, refounded and made houses of Premonstratensian canons in the middle of the century, and St.-Gervais, refounded as a Cistercian priory, dependent on Molesme, in 1137. Just south of Auxerre were the churches of St.-Julien, a convent of Benedictine nuns founded in the seventh century, and the church of St.-Amatre, which became an Augustinian priory in the twelfth century. About eighteen kilometers northeast of Auxerre was the Cistercian abbey of Pontigny, founded in 1114.

The diocese of which Auxerre was the episcopal seat lay in northern Burgundy, in the archdiocese of Sens (see Figure 2). Stretching from the Serein river about fifteen kilometers north of Auxerre to the foothills of the Morvan some seventy-five kilometers to the south, bounded roughly on the east by the Serein and the Yonne, on the west by the Loire, the diocese was primarily contained within the boundaries of the modern department of Yonne but also included small parts of modern Loiret and Nièvre. (Roughly the northern third of the modern department of Yonne is in the old diocese of Sens.) During the French Revolution, the diocese of Auxerre was absorbed into the diocese of Sens.

The Sources

The most important source for the history of the bishops of Auxerre is the collection of their biographies, the *Gesta pontificum Autissiodorensium*. The compilation of this work was originally begun in the ninth century. At that time, brief accounts of the lives of all the bishops of Auxerre since the foundation of the see were written under the direction of Bishop Wala (873–879). Additions were made intermittently until the late thirteenth century, when the series broke off for over two hundred years. Until this period, the series of episcopal biographies is complete, though a

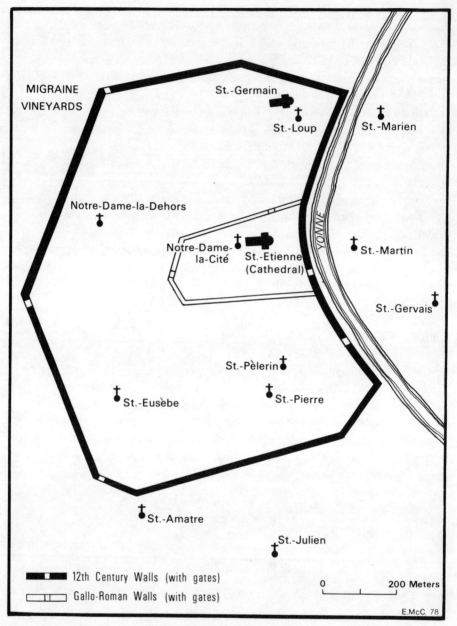

Figure 1. The City of Auxerre

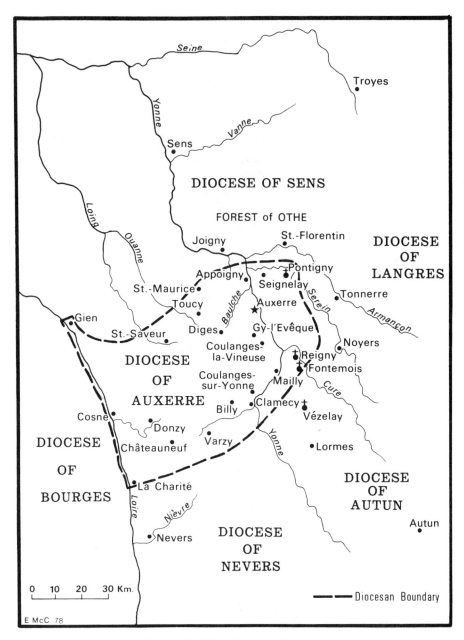

Figure 2. The Diocese of Auxerre

number of them are quite short and some seem to have been written long after the bishop's death. The *Gesta pontificum Autissiodorensium* is preserved as MS 142 of the Bibliothèque d'Auxerre, a twelfth-century copy to which later additions were made, and has been edited by L.-M. Duru. His edition is an accurate and serviceable transcription of the text of the manuscript.[8]

The first *vitae* of the *Gesta pontificum Autissiodorensium* (written in the ninth century) were modeled after the *Liber Pontificalis* of the popes (also known as the *Gesta pontificum Romanorum*), which had first been compiled several centuries earlier.[9] In fact there is evidence that the chapter of Auxerre owned a copy of the *Liber Pontificalis* in the ninth century.[10] These biographies of the popes usually recorded the deeds of men who had carried out their duties well but had no special claim to sainthood. Like the biographies of the *Liber Pontificalis*, the early biographies of the bishops of Auxerre were quite short, often less than 300 words, and they followed a simple chronological framework: first a few sentences on the bishop's geographic and family origins and the length of his time in the see, then an account of his most striking achievements, and finally a brief description of his death. Similar biographies had been composed for the bishops of Metz in the late eighth century and the bishops of Le Mans in the early ninth century, but the biographies written at Auxerre in the late ninth century established a permanent tradition in the see, while the works written elsewhere did not give rise to any continuing record.[11]

8. *Gesta Pontificum Autissiodorensium*, ed. L.-M. Duru, *Bibliothèque historique de l'Yonne* 1 (Auxerre, 1850), 309–509. (Hereafter cited as *Gesta*, with page number.) Pierre Janin prepared a new critical edition of the *Gesta* in 1969 as his thesis at the Ecole des Chartes, but this edition has unfortunately never been published, and I have been unable to obtain a copy of his typescript, in spite of the best efforts of the Bibliothèque of Auxerre and the Midwest Center for Research Libraries.

9. L. Duchesne, ed., *Le Liber pontificalis*, 2 vols. (Paris, 1886–92; repr. 1955). Cyrille Vogel, ed., *Le Liber pontificalis* 3, *Additions et corrections* (Paris, 1957). See also L. Duchesne, *Etude sur le Liber pontificalis* (Paris, 1887), for a discussion of the date, the sources, and authentic texts, and, for a more recent survey, Ottorino Bertolini, "Il 'Liber pontificalis,' " *La storiografia altomedievale*, Settimane di studi del Centro italiano di studi sull'alto medioevo 17 (Spoleto, 1970), 2:387–455.

10. According to Robert-Henri Bautier, "L'historiographie en France aux Xe et XIe siècles," *La storiografia altomedievale*, 2:812. Bautier seems to have based this statement on Janin's unpublished edition.

11. Ibid., pp. 810–11. The brief *Gesta* of the bishops of Metz, composed by Paul the Deacon, are edited in MGH SS 2:261–70. The *Gesta* of the bishops of Le Mans were composed as part of a ninth-century attempt to establish episcopal claims to a great deal of property in Maine: see Walter Goffart, *The Le Mans Forgeries*, Harvard Historical Studies 76 (Cambridge, Mass., 1966), pp. 39–50. Michel Sot has recently studied a number of ninth-century *Gesta* from France, Italy, and Gemany, indicat-

Toward the end of the eleventh century, at a time when no entries were being made in the *Liber Pontificalis*, the biographers of the bishops of Auxerre lengthened their works to at least 1000 words. Around the same time, the sees of Cambrai, Liège, Trier, Toul, Hamburg, and Halberstadt, none of which had produced earlier episcopal biographies, all began to compose *gesta* of their bishops.[12] Though the eleventh-century biographers of Auxerre retained the basic chronological framework of their predecessors, they expanded the section on each bishop's achievements and divided it into several topics, for example, gifts to local monasteries, defense of episcopal castles, and virtuous personal attributes. By the twelfth century it was standard practice for the biographers to organize their material explicitly according to its bearing on separate topics, the separations being indicated by a sentence or two summarizing each section and introducing the next (no actual subheadings were used before the thirteenth century).

Although there is no direct evidence of where the eleventh- and twelfth-century biographers found the pattern for their expanded biographies, the topical (rather than chronological) treatment of their subjects' achievements is similar to the pattern for biography established by Suetonius in the second century. Suetonius arranged his material by topic and divided it with introductory and summary sentences called *divisiones*. His example directly influenced some ecclesiastical as well as secular biographies in the eleventh and twelfth centuries (such as William of Malmesbury's *vita* of St. Wulfstan) and exercised an indirect influence on secular biography through Einhard's *Life of Charlemagne*.[13] The biographers of Auxerre might have found a model in Suetonius for the topical division of their expanded biographies, but they did not adopt his characteristic use of physical description of the subject and verbatim reports of conversation. R. W. Southern has differentiated between four models or patterns that he be-

---

ing the concern in these works for the legitimacy and continuity of the bishops of each see and their possessions: "Historiographie épiscopale et modèle familial en Occident au IXe siècle," *Annales—ESC* 33 (1978), 433–49.

12. Bautier, "L'historiographie en France," pp. 814–15, 829. Contemporary with this flourishing of episcopal biographies on the continent, there developed an Anglo-Saxon tradition of biographies of bishops and abbots, which emphasized the continuity of the see as well as the value of the individual prelates: Antonia Gransden, *Historical Writing in England c. 550 to c. 1307* (Ithaca, 1974), pp. 69, 114–15.

13. G. B. Townend, "Suetonius and His Influence," in *Latin Biography*, ed. T. A. Dorey (London, 1967), pp. 87–98. For Suetonius's influence on ecclesiastical biographies, see D. H. Farmer, "Two Biographies by William of Malmesbury," ibid., pp. 166–67.

lieves influenced medieval biography: the "heroic" model of lives of the early saints, the non-miraculous "commemorative" model, which he traced back as far as the tenth-century *vitae* of the abbots of Cluny, the "secular" model of ancient authors like Suetonius, and the "desert" model of Cassian's lives of the Desert Fathers.[14] The biographies of Auxerre resemble most closely Southern's "commemorative" model, insofar as the authors devoted the bulk of their work to the laudable practical activities of their subjects. Inasmuch as the biographies are structured like the *Liber Pontificalis*, however, they differ from the tenth-century biographies of the abbots of Cluny.

Although the biographers of the bishops of Auxerre sometimes gave their subjects attributes similar to those of contemporary sainted bishops and included a few miracles, the structure of the *vitae* seem to have been only slightly influenced by the hagiographical tradition of the lives of early Christian saints (Southern's "heroic" model). The biographers began with a bishop's election to Auxerre, rather than with an unusual birth and portentous childhood. They described his virtues in a static manner, rather than giving an account of a sudden conversion and arduous penance. They described his activities in a topical, rather than chronological, framework, as mentioned above, though a saint's life usually related his miraculous deeds chronologically. There was nothing comparable in these *vitae* to the form that Charles Altman has seen in saints' lives, where the account begins with the saint as an exception to the old norm and ends with the establishment of a new norm around the saint.[15] The didactic element was slight in the Auxerre biographies; the reader was not urged to imitate the bishop. The biographies also do not seem to have been intended for use in the liturgy, as saints' lives were used, although a biography might have been read on the anniversary of a bishop's death. As there is no record of a contemporary cult of any of these bishops, it is unlikely that any of the biographies were written in order to lay the groundwork for canonization.

Although structurally the *vitae* owed little to the hagiographical tradition, their content was of course closely related; the biographers wrote

14. R. W. Southern, "Traditional Patterns of Biography," in *Saint Anselm and His Biographer: A Study of Monastic Life and Thought, 1059-c. 1130* (Cambridge, Eng., 1963), pp. 320–38.
15. Charles F. Altman, "Two Types of Opposition and the Structure of Latin Saints' Lives," *Medievalia et Humanistica*, n.s. 6 (1975), 8–9. For the topical vs. chronological arrangement of material in biography and saints' lives, see Townend, "Seutonius and His Influence," p. 97. A valuable summary account of *vitae* and *gesta* is provided by Herbert Grundmann, *Geschichtsschreibung im Mittelalter: Gattungen—Epochen—Eigenart* (Göttingen, 1965), pp. 29–45.

with the intention of portraying laudable men. Very little is known about the seven men who wrote the biographies of the twelfth-century bishops of Auxerre, other than that they were canons of the cathedral. All but two of the biographers are anonymous, and scarcely anything beyond their names is known about these two. If they wrote chronicles or literary works besides their biographies, that fact too is unknown. Therefore, their intent and objectives in writing must be inferred from the biographies themselves. Their chief focus was the bishops, but they also included many details of contemporary Burgundian history. As Roger Ray has pointed out, distinctions between medieval church history, regional history, and hagiography are modern artifacts, not a reflection of the broad-sweeping content of a medieval "historia."[16]

Thus, in describing the bishops and their place in local history, the biographers of Auxerre, like hagiographers, found it quite appropriate to go beyond a simple record for posterity of the virtues and practical achievements of their bishops. The lists of gifts to monasteries, of *villae* where the bishop constructed new buildings, or of monasteries reformed to a new order, can all be demonstrated to be accurate whenever the statements in the biographies can be checked against surviving documents. However, the discussions of the bishops' personal qualities owe nothing to the charters, and indeed much archival material survives which the biographers did not use. The biographers selected the most outstanding characteristics and achievements of their subjects to show the power of God in action. They set out to show how well their subjects conformed to God's plan for episcopal activity, and they wrote their works quite consciously influenced by the 250-year tradition of the see that all bishops should have such biographies, written shortly after their deaths.[17]

Additional information about the twelfth-century bishops of Auxerre can be obtained from an independent chronicle composed at Auxerre at the end of the twelfth century and from the documents issued by the bishops themselves. These other sources generally confirm the content of the biographies or give added detail, though they also indicate places where some biographers passed in silence over an entire sphere of episcopal activity—for example a bishop's quarrels with his chapter or other eccle-

16. Roger D. Ray, "Medieval Historiography through the Twelfth Century: Problems and Progress of Research," *Viator* 5 (1974), 35-37.
17. The biographer of Bishop Robert, writing at the end of the eleventh century, described the composition of a biography immediately after each bishop's death as standard practice: "Altissiodorensis ecclesiae non ignobilis consuetudo est, quam cito de seculo migrat ejus episcopus, ilico terminum vitae, sedis introitum, ac precipue bene gesta ipsius conscribere" (*Gesta*, p. 397).

siastics. The general agreement between the biographies and the other sources on most points has led me to conclude that the biographies can be considered factually accurate for points on which there is no other authority. When a major point is mentioned in the other sources but not the biographies, I have tried to establish if there was any particular reason why the biographer should not have mentioned it, although of course the biographers cannot be expected to discuss every administrative act of the bishops for which there is a record.

The chronicle of Robert of St.-Marien was composed around the year 1200 in the Premonstratensian house of St.-Marien of Auxerre, at the urging of Robert's abbot Milo. Robert, a Premonstratensian canon, had less contact with the bishops of Auxerre than did the authors of the *Gesta*. Robert was incorrectly identified by the Abbé Lebeuf in the eighteenth century with one Robert Abolanz, a contemporary cathedral canon, and in some modern works the confusion still persists. It was demonstrated in the nineteenth century that the two Roberts were different and that the chronicle of St.-Marien was composed quite separately from the composition of the *Gesta pontificum Autissiodorensium:* Robert Abolanz appeared in documents of the cathedral chapter as one of its dignitaries for several years after Robert of St.-Marien had died, and there is no evidence that the former ever composed anything.[18]

Robert of St.-Marien's work is a history of the world in the form of annals, in which he arranged events by years and combined details of local history with general events. This old form of historical writing experienced a broad revival in Europe at the beginning of the thirteenth century.[19] The history of the Crusades and of twelfth-century Burgundy make up a large part of Robert's Chronicle. For the later twelfth century, he gave most years a full entry of several hundred words, commenting on virtuous men, heresies, and portents, as well as narrating wars, accessions, and deaths. Robert had brought his chronicle down to his own time when he died in 1212. The original copy of the chronicle is preserved as MS 145 of the Bibliothèque d'Auxerre. Oswald Holder-Egger produced an excellent edition of the twelfth- and thirteenth-century portions of the chronicle; he did not edit the early portion, most of which was copied from previous chronicles and world histories.[20]

---

18. Maximilien Quantin, "Notice sur l'auteur de la Chronique de St.-Marien," *Bulletin de la Société des sciences historiques et naturelles de l'Yonne* 37 (1883), 159–68.
19. Gransden, *Historical Writing*, pp. 318, 519.
20. MGH SS 26:219–87. (Hereafter cited as Robert of St.-Marien, with page numbers.)

The diplomatic sources for the history of the bishops are fuller for the end than for the beginning of the twelfth century. The majority of them are preserved in originals or in medieval copies in series G and H of the Archives départementales de l'Yonne. A great number of episcopal acts concerning the abbey of St.-Germain are preserved in the thirteenth-century Cartulaire de St.-Germain (MS 161 of the Bibliothèque d'Auxerre). There are also some documents preserved in printed form, primarily in *Gallia Christiana*, the *Patrologia Latina*, and Abbé Lebeuf's *Mémoires sur l'histoire d'Auxerre*, for which the originals no longer exist. Many of these were printed from the seventeenth-century transcriptions of Dom Viole (MSS 152–158, Bibliothèque d'Auxerre) and the eighteenth-century editions of Lebeuf. Most of the surviving documents come from the archives of local monasteries. There are almost no surviving records of the internal management of episcopal domains (as distinct from the records of diocesan administration); these records were destroyed in the sixteenth-century Wars of Religion, when the episcopal palace of Regennes, where they were stored, was burned to the ground. The majority of twelfth-century episcopal acts, both those for which originals exist and many of those existing only in late copies, can be conveniently consulted in the three volumes of documents edited by Maximilien Quantin, which go from the early Middle Ages to the mid-thirteenth century.[21] A comparison between the manuscripts and the printed texts indicates that Quantin was an extremely careful editor. Approximately one-fourth of the total number of documents known to have been issued or witnessed by a twelfth-century bishop of Auxerre have not been printed but may be consulted in the original copies at the Archives de l'Yonne.[22]

Spirituality and Administration

In the following pages I will discuss the changing role of the bishop in twelfth-century Auxerre by examining the activities and achievements of each of the seven bishops in turn. The chief focus of each chapter will be the bishop as revealed in his biography: what he did and what his biographer thought he ought to have done. The picture will be filled in by the

21. Maximilien Quantin, ed., *Cartulaire général de l'Yonne*, 2 vols. (Auxerre, 1854–60); *Recueil de pièces pour faire suite au Cartulaire général de l'Yonne* (Auxerre, 1873). (Hereafter these three volumes will be referred to as Quantin 1, 2, 3, with document and page numbers.)

22. These documents are edited in Constance B. Bouchard, "The Bishop of Auxerre in the Twelfth Century: Spirituality and Administration" (Ph.D. dissertation, University of Chicago, 1976), Appendix I, "Previously Unedited Documents of the Bishops of Auxerre," pp. 294–382.

13

details given in the bishop's charters and, for the last two bishops, by the chronicle of Robert of St.-Marien.

Each bishop will be discussed in terms of his "spirituality" and "administration." The biographers always distinguished between these two categories. The word "spirituality," however, is not theirs. I use it as a broad term to describe what the individual biographers refer to as "holiness" or "virtue." In this sense the term has come to be accepted by modern scholars such as André Vauchez, who defines spirituality as the religious dimension of the inner life, that which tends toward God.[23] Information on a bishop's spirituality—the presence or absence of spirituality appropriate for a bishop, and the way his spirituality was expressed—comes almost entirely from the biographies. A section at the beginning of each account is devoted to the bishop's virtues, and in most cases the author mentions these virtues again when they are manifested in particular acts of the bishop.

The bulk of all the biographies is given to the practical achievements of the bishops, which the biographers call *administratio*. In most of the biographies a distinction is made between the bishop's care for the local houses of his diocese and his care for the temporal possessions adhering to the episcopal office, that is, between "diocesan" and "temporal" administration. These two categories were sometimes treated independently: for example, the biographer of Hugh of Noyers called his subject outstanding in temporal affairs (the defense of episcopal property) but remiss in diocesan *administratio*. Other episcopal administrative activities included relations with the cathedral chapter and (for the last two bishops) suppression of heresy. Some biographers placed these topics in the section on diocesan administration, others in the section on temporal administration. In all cases, the details of administrative activities given in the biographies can be supplemented with the evidence in the documents.

In describing their subjects' spirituality and administrative achievements, the biographers attempted to present pictures of men who conformed well to their ideal of what a bishop should be. There was no fixed ideal, however, other than the very general one that a good bishop would demonstrate holiness of life and take proper care of his diocese and episcopal property; the biographer's understanding of the ideal role for a bishop seems to have been based largely on his reaction to what his subject actually did. To indicate that his bishop was an excellent one, each biographer compared him to men in the Bible or to the Church Fathers. The pseudo-Pauline epistles 1 Timothy and Titus described a good bishop

23. André Vauchez, *La spiritualité du moyen âge occidental, VIIIe–XIIe siècles* (Paris, 1975), p. 5.

as one who was chaste, hospitable, temperate, courteous, and not given to brawling. The *Pastoral Care* of Gregory the Great expanded this brief list with a discussion of how a bishop should treat his flock and especially the humility he should show. The Pauline and Gregorian descriptions of episcopal virtue dominated early medieval discussions of what sort of man a bishop should be, and they influenced the lists of virtues given by some of the biographers of Auxerre. In addition, the biographers drew parallels between their subjects and such highly respected figures as Augustine, Ambrose, Jerome, St. Martin, Phineas, St. Paul, and Christ.

The following pages should demonstate that there was no unchanging standard to which all the twelfth-century biographers expected their subjects to conform. Rather, within the general framework of episcopal spirituality and administration, there are definite shifts evident in the biographies—paralleling shifts in the emphases seen in the documents—in the role of the bishops of Auxerre. These changes were a part of the broader twelfth-century concern for finding the best form of the religious life and determining how this life related to the exercise of authority. The evidence for this concern may be seen in the change from the first half of the twelfth century, when popes and French bishops were often originally monks from reformed houses, to the last half, when pontiffs were generally administrators and lawyers; in debates over the relative advantage of the active and contemplative lives; in the resignations of some abbots and bishops from their administrative positions to seek a deeper spirituality; in the increasing attempt to submit all religious enthusiasts to ecclesiastical rule and to prosecute them as heretics if they did not submit; and in the ever-growing emphasis put on preaching and ministering. Spirituality had been almost completely identified with monasticism at the beginning of the twelfth century; by the end of the century there were multiple perceptions of the spiritual life, with different religious goals for different orders of society.[24] The following pages on the bishops of Auxerre are intended to shed new light on one aspect of the changing concepts of spirituality and administrative duties during the course of the twelfth century.

24. For the decline in the number of French bishops, see Bouchard, "Origins of Bishops," pp. 287–90. For the debate over the active and contemplative lives, see the *Libellus de diversis ordinibus et professionibus qui sunt in aecclesia*, ed. Giles Constable and B. Smith (Oxford, 1972), especially Constable's introduction, p. xii. For the increasing emphasis on regularizing religious enthusiasts, see Herbert Grundmann, *Religiöse Bewegungen im Mittelalter*, 2nd ed. (Hildesheim, 1961), pp. 41–50. For the development of different religious goals for different orders of society, see Vauchez, *La spiritualité du moyen âge*, pp. 6, 84–89. See also Giles Constable, "Twelfth-Century Spirituality and the Late Middle Ages," *Medieval and Renaissance Studies* 5 (1969), 40–42.

I

HUMBAUD AND THE ESTABLISHMENT
OF REGULAR ORDER

When Humbaud (1092–1114) was consecrated as bishop of Auxerre, the bishopric had just escaped from the direct tutelage of the local secular authorities. His predecessor Robert, son of the count of Nevers, was count of Auxerre in his own right. Robert had been preceded by the son of the viscount of Nevers. Humbaud had to struggle against rival claimants for three years after his election before he felt secure enough to leave the city and have his hard-won office confirmed by papal consecration.

The Gregorian reform had touched Auxerre fifteen years earlier, when the papal legate Hugh of Die investigated Robert at the Council of Autun (1077) to determine if he had received investiture from the king—he had not—and censured him for having been ordained before the canonical age, though Robert was allowed to keep his office.[1] But, at the beginning of Humbaud's pontificate, the Gregorian reform had had little other effect on Auxerre. The once distinguished abbey of St.-Germain had fallen into disrepute under an abbot accused of scandalous behavior. Many local churches, including the cathedral, were badly dilapidated. The religious enthusiasm that spread monastic reform and new houses and orders across France in the late eleventh and early twelfth century had not yet reached Auxerre.

This situation changed during Humbaud's pontificate. His anonymous biographer described ecclesiastical reform and the foundation of new houses as the chief characteristics of his years in office. All but 500 words of his 2300-word biography are a description of Humbaud's vigorous program of recovering episcopal property from lay hands and introducing regular life into the local monasteries (the other 500 words are the desciption of Humbaud's family, election, and virtues). After a few introductory sentences on how Humbaud became bishop, the biographer launched into his discussion of the many reforms the bishop effected. In each case, he began by describing the deplorable state in which Humbaud found ecclesiastical lands and edifices at the beginning of his pontificate—church territory de-

---

1. Mansi 20:488. Charles-Joseph Hefele, *Historie des conciles*, trans. and aug. H. Leclercq, 5, 1 (Paris, 1912), 224. (Hereafter cited as Hefele-Leclercq, with volume and page numbers.)

populated by "tyrants," the cathedral roof in decay, episcopal fields un-cultivated, and the local monks living without a rule—and then said that the "wise and prudent" bishop quickly effected remedies. He next de-scribed the favorable condition in which Humbaud left the diocese—tyrants ousted, the cathedral reroofed, fields restored to fertility, and new houses of regular monks established—though he gave only a few details on the methods the bishop used to achieve these happy results. The biographer clearly considered Humbaud an excellent bishop, whose ability was evi-dent in the prosperous condition of the churches of Auxerre at the time the biography was written.

Humbaud came from a noble family of the Auxerrois region. His biog-rapher gave the names of his parents, Humbaud and Adela, and said that they were of noble (*nobilis*) stock, but nothing more is known about his family. At the time of his election, Humbaud had been a canon of the Auxerre cathedral chapter for at least forty years, having been made a canon under Bishop Heribert (1040–1052), and he was serving as dean, the highest office in the chapter.

The details of his election are somewhat obscure; not even the year is sure. Since Humbaud is known to have died in 1114, shortly after partici-pating in the foundation of Pontigny, and since his biographer assigned him an episcopate of 22 years and 4 months, it is logical to assume that he was elected in 1092. His biographer said that he was consecrated by Urban II in Milan; if so, his consecration probably took place in 1095, the only year the pope is known to have been in Milan.[2] That three years inter-vened between Humbaud's election and the time when all interested parties agreed to accept him, allowing papal confirmation, appears to be confirmed in the biography of his predecessor. The author reports that three years of confusion elapsed after Robert's death before the chapter could agree on a successor.[3] Humbaud's biographer mentioned no dissent, only describing the election as taking place in the prescribed manner *a clero et populo civitatis*, a conventional and imprecise phrase that need not mean that his election was free from controversy or from the influence of the local nobility. If any of the nobility did try to influence the choice of a successor to Robert, the count's son, they were not successful in ob-taining a bishop favorable to their interests, for, once he was consecrated, Humbaud gave much of his attention to forcing local lords to give up the rights and property he believed they had usurped from the bishopric.

---

2. Quantin 1.122, pp. 228–30. *Gesta*, p. 402. Philip Jaffé, *Regesta pontificum Roman-orum ab condita ecclesia ad annum post Christum natum MCXCVIII*, ed. and aug. Wilhelm Wattenbach, 1 (Leipzig, 1885), 679.

3. *Gesta*, p. 397.

Regularity and Reform

Throughout the biography there is a repeated use of the term "regular" (*regularis* and its cognates). The biographer did not define "regularity" precisely, but he generally used the term, as did most ecclesiastical reformers of his time, to mean the establishment of the form of monastic life in which the brothers followed a strict rule of conduct and lived in common without any personal property.[4] He also used it in a wider sense, to mean general order and quiet in the diocese. When describing Humbaud's establishment of regularity, the biographer always indicated that the bishop had restored conditions to their original, prosperous state, and, further, that he introduced improvements not before seen. Throughout his description of this reform, the biographer, a cathedral canon, gave chief emphasis to the property of the bishop and of the cathedral and its canons, rather than to that of other diocesan churches.

The biographer began his description of Humbaud's reforms with an account of "tyrannical" laymen who had seized and were destroying episcopal property. The usurped property was located at Toucy, Varzy, and Cosne (located respectively 22, 50, and 65 kilometers from Auxerre), where the bishops of Auxerre had long had castles.[5] The biographer called the usurping knights *casati ecclesiae*, a term indicating that they had held these lands in direct tenure from the church. Humbaud, "harmless and wise" like the dove and the serpent (*simplex ac prudens*, as Jesus commanded his followers to be, Matt. 10.16), and "confident of the power of God," took back the property from the usurpers with "ecclesiastical justice." Henceforth he kept the land in his own hands, rather than granting it in fief to other knights who might again try to appropriate it for their own.[6]

The biographer emphasized the dependent nature of the *casati ecclesiae* who had usurped episcopal land, but he also showed Humbaud defending his rights against the most powerful laymen of the diocese. In fact, one of the "knights" was Geoffrey, lord of Donzy, who controlled several castles and a great deal of land in the southern and western part of the diocese. Humbaud also pressed his rights against the count of Joigny, whose small county lay a short distance north of Auxerre. According to custom, the

4. Jean-François Lemarignier, Jean Gaudemet, and Guillaume Mollat, *Institutions ecclésiastiques*, Histoire des institutions françaises au moyen âge 3 (Paris, 1962), pp. 132–34.
5. By 849 they had already had land at Toucy and Cosne for many years: Quantin 1.31, pp. 61–63. They had had an episcopal castle at Varzy from at least the tenth century: *Gesta*, p. 391.
6. *Gesta*, pp. 402–03.

bishop of Auxerre owed this count a payment or *consuetudo* of 300 solidi a year for the episcopal castle at Appoigny, which lay on the border of the counties of Auxerre and Joigny. Although Humbaud was not able to eliminate this payment, the biographer recorded that he had it decreased from 300 to 260 solidi a year.[7] In addition, the biographer indicated that Humbaud was able to wring concessions from the most powerful secular lord of the region, the count of Auxerre, Nevers, and Tonnerre.

The family of the hereditary counts of Nevers emerged from obscurity at the end of the tenth century (see Figure 3). By the middle of the eleventh century, members of this family had made themselves counts of Auxerre and Tonnerre as well (successive counts had married the sister of King Robert II and the heiress of Tonnerre).[8] These three counties stayed in one family until the end of the twelfth century. The counts usually styled themselves simply as counts of Nevers, both because this was the most important county and because younger brothers were sometimes made titular counts of Tonnerre and Auxerre (the three counties were always reunited at the end of each generation because the younger brothers almost never married or had legitimate children). The county of Tonnerre was held in fief from the duke of Burgundy, but, since the early eleventh century, Auxerre and Nevers had been fiefs held directly from the king.

At the time of Humbaud's consecration, the count of Nevers was William I, father of Humbaud's predecessor Robert. William I died in 1098 and was succeeded by his grandson William II as count of Nevers, Auxerre, and Tonnerre. The biographer recorded that Humbaud quickly persuaded the new count to grant him a charter guaranteeing that he would no longer exercise the evil custom (*prava consuetudo*) by which the counts had seized the house and furnishings of each bishop as soon as he died; William I had undoubtedly exercised this custom during the three years of confusion between bishop Robert's death and Humbaud's consecration. A few years later, when the bishop of Nevers died, William II promised the new bishop, in a charter similar to the one he had given Humbaud, that he would no longer seize episcopal goods when the see fell vacant.[9] The custom that William repudiated was the *ius spolii*, originally the right of the king to the lands belonging to a bishopric, including rights to taxes, income, and justice, during a vacancy, a right claimed since Carolingian times. In the

7. Ibid., p. 405.
8. "Origo et historia brevis Nivernensium comitum," ed. R. B. C. Huygens, *Monumenta Vizeliacensia*, Corpus Christianorum Continuatio Mediaevalis 42 (Turnhout, 1976), pp. 235-39.
9. For Auxerre, see *Gesta*, p. 405. For Nevers, see René de Lespinasse, ed., *Cartulaire de Saint-Cyr de Nevers* (Nevers, 1916), pp. 181-82, no. 108.

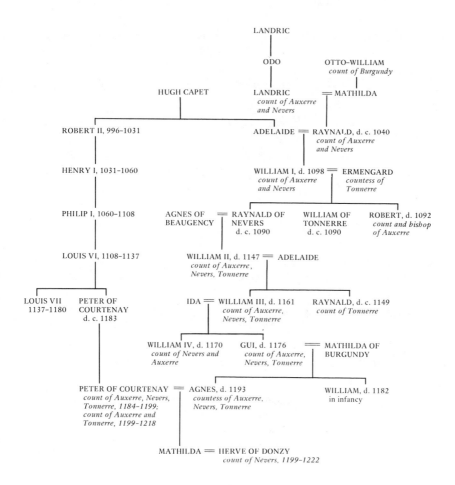

Figure 3. The Counts of Auxerre, Nevers, and Tonnerre

eleventh century, when French royal power diminished, this right was usually exercised by the local nobility.[10]

The biographer gave the impression that Humbaud had no further trouble from the count, although the documents show that in fact the bishop and the count continued to quarrel over certain lands near Auxerre. The letters of Ivo of Chartres indicate that Humbaud once wrote Ivo, who was compiling a new collection of texts of canon law, to ask for some arguments and citations he could use against the count at court. Ivo sent him only a stiff reprimand for taking cases involving ecclesiastical property before a secular judge.[11] The standard procedure would have been to take the case before the archbishop or before ecclesiastical arbiters agreed upon by both parties; this is probably the type of procedure to which the biographer referred when he said Humbaud recovered land from tyrannical knights through "ecclesiastical justice," the type Ivo preferred Humbaud to use. As well as overstating Humbaud's success against the count, the biographer gave the impression that Humbaud never required the assistance of the count in any of his other cases. In fact, in 1110, when Humbaud drew up a charter threatening excommunication for the lords of Toucy if they did not give up their claims on the property of the abbey of Fleury-sur-Loire that was located in the diocese of Auxerre, Count William and his knights were present and declared themselves ready to help enforce the charter.[12]

After describing Humbaud's reclamation of episcopal lands and rights from usurping laymen, the biographer turned to his improvements to the cathedral. He said the the edifice was "dilapidated" and "worn out" (*vetustate consumpta atque dilapsa*) and that Humbaud's many great works of improvement made evident how "piously, kindly, and wisely" he behaved toward the church and the men put under his care.[13] The Romanesque cathedral had been built about seventy-five years earlier by Bishop Hugh of Chalon. Humbaud, whom his biographer described as motivated by the words of the Psalmist, "Lord, I have loved the habitation of thy house and the place where thy honor dwelleth" (Psalm 26.8), put on a new roof (the old one leaked), replaced the wooden towers with nonflammable stone towers, opened up new windows by the altars, installed new candelabra, acquired some decorative hangings embroidered with

10. Jean Gaudemet, *La collation par le roi de France des bénéfices vacants en régale des origines à la fin du XIVe siècle* (Paris, 1935), p. 3.
11. Ivo of Chartres, Letter 241, PL 162:248–49.
12. Quantin 1.117, pp. 220–21.
13. *Gesta*, pp. 403–04: "Hic igitur quam pie erga ecclesiam sibi susceptam, quam benigne ac prudenter erga subditos sese habuit, preclara ejus facta demonstrant."

kings and lions for use on feast days, bought a number of liturgical books and vestments, and had both the ceiling of the church and the crypts below it decorated with liturgical pictures. A picture of Christ Triumphant, on horseback and carrying a sword, accompanied by the symbols of the four Evangelists (cf. Rev. 19.11-17), which apparently dates from these renovations, may still be seen in the crypt. It seems appropriate that Humbaud, who brought spiritual warfare against those who usurped the rights and property of the church, should have had this particular representation of Christ in his cathedral crypt, a representation believed unique in contemporary French art.[14] The biographer, who summarized Humbaud's improvements by saying he had "ennobled" the cathedral with honors (*honoribus nobilitavit*), added that Humbaud would have done even more for the cathedral had not the devil, working through the agency of the "tyrants" who had usurped episcopal lands, inflicted numerous injuries on episcopal goods. Though he here suggested that Humbaud's triumph against the "tyrants" was not as complete as he had indicated a few sentences earlier, it is clear that Humbaud's repairs to the cathedral were very extensive. The biographer ended this section by mentioning that the bishop completely rebuilt and rededicated the church of Notre-Dame-la-Cité, which stood close to the cathedral, and reroofed Notre-Dame-la-Dehors, which stood outside the city walls.[15]

In repairing the cathedral, Humbaud did not neglect the welfare of those clerics responsible for services there, the chapter of the cathedral canons. The biographer, a canon himself, recorded that Humbaud, in order to increase the level of the canons' prebends, gave them the revenues of three churches he had taken away from laymen and promised them the revenues of a fourth, but died before he could obtain it from the laymen who held it.[16]

The biographer said little about the composition of the chapter, but details can be gained from existing chapters. There were almost fifty canons at this time,[17] most of whom were in minor orders and filled no other ecclesiastical office, although the bishop of Nevers and the abbot of the house of St.-Amatre, just south of Auxerre, were also listed as members of the chapter. Like all French cathedral canons, the members of the chap-

14. René Louis, *Autessiodurum Christianum: Les églises d'Auxerre des origines au XIme siècle* (Paris, 1952), p. 122.

15. *Gesta*, p. 404.

16. Ibid.

17. They are all listed in a charter of about 1100. Jean Lebeuf, *Mémoires concernant l'histoire civile et ecclésiastique d'Auxerre*, ed. and aug. Ambroise Challe and Maximilien Quantin, 4 (Auxerre, 1855), 29.

ter of Auxerre were responsible for services in the cathedral, the election of new bishops (who often came from among their number), and the administration of that part of the cathedral's patrimony which was under their control.

The head of the chapter was the dean, elected by the chapter. Humbaud held this office before his election. He was succeeded as dean by one Frodon, perhaps the same Frodon who wrote the biography of Humbaud's predecessor Robert (written during Humbaud's pontificate).[18] Second only in importance to the dean was the provost, appointed by the bishop, responsible for overseeing the administration of the chapter's lands and other temporal possessions. Other officers included the archdeacon, responsible for the other churches of the diocese in the bishop's absence; the treasurer, sometimes known as the chamberlain; the cantor, responsible for services in the cathedral; the chancellor, responsible for the archives and the production of charters; the cellarer; the school-master; and the sacristan.[19]

Humbaud, who appointed all the capitular officers except the dean, chose one Ulger to be his provost, a man called his nephew in the cathedral necrology.[20] This appointment is the only event in the chapter's affairs on which the biographer gives any details; he reproduces the letter of Pope Paschal II confirming Ulger's possession of the provostship.[21] Though Ulger is not known to have played a significant part in the affairs of the diocese during Humbaud's lifetime, he tried unsucessfully to have himself elected as Humbaud's successor. Since the biographer, writing under Humbaud's successor, described Ulger favorably, he may have been a member of Ulger's faction (see Chapter II).

The biographer at any rate indicated in his work that he always supported Bishop Humbaud and his policies. After describing the bishop's reclamation of property from lay hands and his gifts to the cathedral and the chapter, he described in detail the many improvements he made to episcopal property: "for the utility and advantage of bishops of Auxerre he in his wisdom acquired much good property with great labor." Thus he noted that Humbaud bought for 30 pounds the agricultural *villa* of Les

18. *Gesta*, p. 401. Quantin 1.117, p. 221.
19. For the composition of French chapters and the specific duties of the officers, see Lemarignier, Gaudemet, and Mollat, *Institutions ecclésiastiques*, pp. 188–92; and Gabriel LeBras, *Institutions ecclésiastiques de la Chrétienté médiévale*, Histoire de l'église depuis les origines jusqu'à nos jours 12 (Paris, 1959–64), pp. 376–94.
20. Auguste Longnon, Alexandre Vidier, and Léon Mirot, eds., *Obituaires de la province de Sens* 3, *Diocèses d'Orléans, d'Auxerre et de Nevers* (Paris, 1909), p. 324.
21. *Gesta*, p. 407.

Laurents, 25 kilometers south of Auxerre, adjoining property he already owned, restored disused vineyards to fertility at Auxerre, Appoigny (10 kilometers north of Auxerre), and Gy-l'Evêque (9 kilometers south of Auxerre), set a new mill in the Yonne, acquired new serfs (*servi et ancillae*), constructed new episcopal houses at Gy, Cosne, and Toucy, and rebuilt the fortifications of the castle at Appoigny. In the diocese of Auxerre, as in all French dioceses, the episcopal patrimony consisted of pieces of land widely separated; the biographer indicated that Humbaud's care extended to all of it.[22]

The prominent place that the biographer gave to Humbaud's defense of and improvements to episcopal and capitular property indicates that he considered these activities the bishop's most noteworthy achievements. Only after an 1100-word description of Humbaud's accomplishments in these areas did the biographer give a relatively brief (420-word) description of his reform of the monastic and canonical life of the diocese. This section is introduced by an apology—"And we ought not to have kept silent on this"—and interrupted in the middle by the text of two papal letters, one confirming Humbaud's possessions and the other confirming provost Ulger in his capitular office. Such an emphasis on preservation of rights and property, even at the expense of a discussion of ecclesiastical reform throughout the diocese, is common in contemporary biographies of late eleventh- and early twelfth-century bishops. Preservation or extension of rights could even be considered a bishop's sacred duty by the bishop and his biographer; Anselm of Canterbury, in spite of his own disinclination for the temporal affairs of his diocese, is recorded as having said, "I would not dare to appear before the judgment-seat of God with the rights of my see diminished."[23]

But surviving documents indicate that Humbaud played a much broader role in the affairs of the diocesan churches and indeed the wider church than the brevity of the biographer's account might suggest. Though perhaps not as concrete as the fiefs he recovered, fields he bought and cultivated, or roofs he replaced, the reformed rules that he established at local houses and the synods that he attended were at least as important contributions to religious life in Auxerre.

22. Ibid., pp. 404–06. The wide distribution of episcopal property at Auxerre may partly be due to the fact that much of the patrimony of the cathedral had been acquired from the early bishops of the see, who came from all over the region and generally left their family property to the church. Gabriel LaBras, "L'organisation du diocèse d'Auxerre à l'époque mérovingienne," *Mémoires de la Société pour l'histoire du droit et des institutions bourguignons* 5 (1938), 9.
23. R. W. Southern, *Western Society and the Church in the Middle Ages* (Harmondsworth, Eng., 1970), pp. 185–88.

The biographer began his account of Humbaud's diocesan administration with a report on the restoration of regularity to the local monastery of St.-Germain, an almost classic case of a house fallen from a strict rule. St.-Germain was a Benedictine house dating from the sixth century, which had long been noted for its school, especially outstanding in the ninth century. It had already been reformed once around the year 990, when Abbot Maiolus of Cluny sent one of his monks to become the abbot of St.-Germain and revive its strict observance, which had lapsed during the invasions of Vikings and Magyars during the tenth century.[24] At the end of the eleventh century, the house again clearly needed reformation; the matter crystalized at the time of Humbaud's consecration, when the abbot was accused of leading a scandalous life. The details of the reform of this house can be reconstructed from Humbaud's biography, from a few comments in the contemporary biography of the first abbot of the house after its reform, from the documents issued by the pope and several members of the local nobility, and from a thirteenth-century history of the abbots of St.-Germain, which accords in all points with the documents and may incorporate a lost twelfth-century source.[25]

Humbaud's first known act as bishop was to ask Pope Urban II, at the 1096 Council of Nîmes, to depose Abbot Guibert of St.-Germain. He went straight to the pope in this affair as he had gone straight to him for his consecration, bypassing the archbishop in each case. He may have decided not to consult his archbishop because the sitting archbishop of Sens was Richer (1062–1097), who had been severely reprimanded by Hugh of Die for his own scandalous life, thus hardly the man for Humbaud to consult in his pursuit of canonical regularity.[26] The pope deposed the abbot at once and refused to reinstate him, despite his pleas. Slackened zeal was a common problem in the older monasteries of France around the year 1100;[27] Urban II was distressed by clerical abuses and continued the Gregorian program of eradicating them wherever he found them.

Humbaud's biographer gave a very summary account of how St.-Germain was reformed to a new order after Guibert's deposition: he simply said that Urban granted the bishop the right henceforth to choose the

24. *Gesta*, pp. 382–83.
25. Ibid., pp. 406, 410. Urban II, Letter 286, PL 151:538–39. Quantin 2.36, pp. 37–38. Auguste Bernard and Alexandre Bruel, eds., *Recueil des chartes de l'abbaye de Cluny* 5 (Paris, 1894), 209–10, no. 3859. *De gestibus abbatum S. Germani*, ed. Philippe Labbe, *Novae bibliothecae manuscriptorum librorum* 1 (Paris, 1657), 577.
26. For Richer's scandalous behavior, see Mansi 20:488.
27. Guibert de Nogent, writing in the early twelfth century, described slackened zeal as a frequent concern: *De vita sua* 1.8, ed. Georges Bourgin (Paris, 1907), pp. 22–24.

26

abbot of the house and assure that regular order was maintained there.[28] Other sources, however, indicate that the situation was more complicated. According to the thirteenth-century account written at St.-Germain, the pope suggested to Humbaud that he select a new abbot from among the monks of Cluny, Chaise-Dieu, or Marmoutiers, all houses of renowned regularity of life;[29] Cluny, where Urban II himself had been a monk, seems to have been the only one of the three seriously considered. There was, however, some delay in establishing a Cluniac abbot. The majority of houses living under a Cluniac rule at this time were priories, houses directly dependent on Cluny without an abbot of their own.[30] Abbot Hugh of Cluny sent his own prior to St.-Germain to head the monastery, but Humbaud would not accept him when he learned that as a Cluniac priory St.-Germain would no longer owe obedience to the bishop. Meanwhile a certain Robert, a shadowy figure who was probably one of the monks of St.-Germain, held the office of abbot.

A compromise was reached about 1099, after Robert's death, by the pope, Bishop Humbaud, Count William of Auxerre and Nevers, his viscount Walter, Abbot Hugh of Cluny, and Count Stephen of Blois, who held the advocacy of St.-Germain in fief from the duke of Burgundy. Abbot Hugh was asked to send a monk to Auxerre who would become the abbot of St.-Germain, obedient to the bishop, and who would establish the institutes of Cluny there. The relative authority of the bishop of Auxerre and the abbot of Cluny in the choice of future abbots of St.-Germain was left unclear. Around 1100, a group of monks came to Auxerre from Cluny under the direction of Hugh of Montaigu, nephew of Abbot Hugh of Cluny, who had been absolved of his ecclesiastical obedience to his uncle and would be the new abbot of St.-Germain.[31]

In spite of the part played by the pope, the abbot of Cluny, two counts, and a viscount in establishing Cluniac monks at St.-Germain, as

---

28. *Gesta*, p. 406: ". . . a prelibato Urbano papa secundo in concilio Nemausansi obtinere meruit quatinus Autissiodorensis episcopus in eodem monasterio abbatem in perpetuum, Deo disponente, poneret, et regulari ordine ecclesiam eandem ordinare curaret."

29. Marmoutiers, like Cluny, was the mother house of a large number of priories in which a strictly regulated monastic life was led. Chaise-Dieu, exempt from episcopal control like Cluny, had had most of the nearby monasteries of southern France affiliated with it by Gregory VII. Lemarignier, Gaudemet, and Mollat, *Institutions ecclésiastiques*, pp. 115, 119–20.

30. Noreen Hunt, *Cluny under Saint Hugh, 1049–1109* (London, 1967), p. 165.

31. Although none of the relevant charters are dated, it seems certain that the monks from Cluny came to Auxerre in 1100, as a charter dated 1104 refers to their having been there four years: Quantin 2.39, p. 43.

shown by contemporary charters, Humbaud's biographer described the bishop alone as restoring regular life in the abbey. He did not even mention Cluny and placed the restoration of regular order in the context of the restoration of episcopal control over St.-Germain, "submitted to us by ancient kings of France."[32] Although the biographer was certainly overstating the case in making Humbaud solely responsible for returning St.-Germain to regular life, to some extent his description of Humbaud acting out of individual initiative is justified: Humbaud himself, not some papal legate, discovered the irregularities at St.-Germain, and he was the driving force behind the whole prolonged process of settlement.

The deposition of the scandalous abbot of St.-Germain, ultimately leading to the establishment of Cluniac monks there, was Humbaud's first known act as bishop; one of his last, in 1114, was the foundation of the monastery of Pontigny, the second daughter house of Cîteaux, on land to the northeast of Auxerre that had been given by one of the cathedral canons.[33] The biographer again gave Humbaud the entire credit for choosing the new abbot and did not even mention Cîteaux.

After his descriptions of the establishment of these two houses, which together begin the section on diocesan administration, the biographer listed several other houses which Humbaud either founded or reformed between 1100 and 1114. Shortly after 1100 he established a rule for the monks of Fontemois, a house 28 kilometers southeast of Auxerre that had grown up around two hermits living there. The biographer did not identify the rule that Humbaud gave the monks, but the increasingly numerous small groups of hermits and ascetics in France at this time often became a source of scandal unless submitted to some regular discipline.[34] The biographer also reported that Humbaud established canons regular at two churches of Auxerre, St.-Pierre and St.-Eusèbe, both located a short distance outside the old city walls.[35] The canons regular which he described as settling in these churches represented a form of life that became very common in

32. *Gesta*, p. 406: ". . . monasterium Sancti Germani ab antiquis Francie regibus ecclesie nostre sublatum. . . ."
33. Ibid. Quantin 1.122, pp. 228–30. Robert of St.-Marien, p. 230.
34. *Gesta*, p. 406. Quantin 1.109, pp. 208–10. Jean Leclercq, "The Monastic Crisis of the Eleventh and Twelfth Centuries," *Cluniac Monasticism in the Central Middle Ages*, ed. Noreen Hunt (London, 1971), pp. 226–27. Giles Constable has indicated the continued presence of eremetical elements in all cenobitic houses that developed from an eremetical base; though a bishop might give a group of hermits a rule, they were not thus transformed from one type of spiritual life to another: "The Study of Monastic History Today," in *The Reconstruction of Medieval History*, ed. Vaclav Mudroch and G. S. Couse (Montreal, 1974), pp. 30–31.
35. *Gesta*, pp. 406–08.

twelfth-century France. Canons regular, like monks, lived under a rule of common life and property—a rule based on several treatises of St. Augustine rather than Benedict's *Regula*. In most cases—not all—canons differed from monks in that they were organized for the purposes of performing the holy office and caring for souls as well as carrying out the liturgy in the privacy of the cloister.[36] The biographer gave a great deal of attention to the establishment of canons of an approved (*probabilis*) life in St.-Eusèbe, which had been elevated from a simple parish church to a priory by Humbaud's predecessor Robert and which Humbaud now submitted to a strict rule. It was important for the biographer, a cathedral canon, that there be no scandal connected with St.-Eusèbe, for by force of long tradition the cathedral canons and their servants were buried in this church's graveyard. He gave extensive details on the agreement Humbaud reached with the brothers of St.-Eusèbe by which they would celebrate mass for a year after the death of each canon in return for receiving the income from his prebend for that time.[37]

The biographer's survey of Humbaud's establishment of a rule at different religious houses covered two abbeys, one old, one new, one group of hermits and ascetics, and two bodies of canons regular. He said that these actions were examples of the bishop's many outstanding deeds (*insignia*), but he does not seem to have found it necessary to list individually each regular foundation, for another such foundation, unmentioned by the biographer, is known from Humbaud's documents: the house of Crisenon. This house, which had been under the direct control of the lords of Toucy since its establishment as a priory in the early eleventh century, was submitted by the bishop to the rule of Molesme after he had received it from the lord of Toucy, who was leaving for Jerusalem.[38]

As well as giving a representative list of the houses Humbaud reformed to a regular order, the biographer indicated the bishop's concern for the churches of the diocese by saying that he restored to these churches the

---

36. Luc Verheijen, *Le règle de Saint Augustin*, 2 vols. (Paris, 1967). Caroline W. Bynum has emphasized the similarities in the spiritual lives of twelfth-century monks and canons: "The Spirituality of Regular Canons in the Twelfth Century: A New Approach," *Medievalia et Humanistica*, n.s. 4 (1973), 3–5. She was influenced in large part by the work of Charles Dereine; see especially his "Chanoines," *Dictionnaire d'histoire et de géographie ecclésiastique* 12:376–404 [1953]. See also Leclercq, "Monastic Crisis," p. 223; Constable, "The Study of Monastic History," pp. 32–33; and Jacques Hourlier, *L'âge classique, 1140–1378: Les réligieux*, Histoire du droit et des institutions de l'église en Occident 10 (Paris, 1973), pp. 81–89.
37. *Gesta*, p. 408.
38. Quantin 1.103, 115, pp. 199–200, 218–19.

ecclesiastical income which had previously passed into lay hands. In these deeds, he said, the bishop was motivated both by "love for the divine office and for ecclesiastical order" and by the (apocryphal) saying of the martyred Pope Stephen that "no layman, even if pious, should possess any ecclesiastical goods."[39] He briefly described a synod which Humbaud held, in which he forbade ecclesiastics to make annual payments to local laymen. As a demonstration of the synod's success, the biographer recorded the disposition of the parish churches which the bishop recovered from laymen: he gave several to his chapter, several to St.-Eusèbe and to the Cluniac house of La Charité, located at the far southern end of the diocese, and kept at least two others, the parish churches located in the episcopal castles of Varzy and Cosne, for himself and for future bishops of Auxerre.[40] Only in passing, at the end of his work, did the biographer indicate that this synod did not immediately and completely end all lay control of churches and ecclesiastical income. As another example of Humbaud's being "harmless as a dove and wise as a serpent," he described a situation in which a layman charged that he had been harmed by the property claims of ecclesiastics and tried to recover what he considered his own. In such a case, according to the biographer, Humbaud usually tried to suppress the layman's claim, rather than having it arbitrated before ecclesiastical judges as would have been the ordinary procedure, or else quietly paid the layman to give up his claims, "lest there be a scandal in the church."[41] Certainly the laymen were not as willing as the biographer had earlier indicated to give up church property, and indeed a great deal must have remained in lay hands throughout Humbaud's episcopate, since his successors continued to recover ecclesiastical income and property from the local nobility.

The biographer's descriptions of the reform of local houses and the synod at which laymen were forbidden to hold ecclesiastical property give a central place to the wisdom and initiative of the bishop. It is indicative of the importance the biographer gave to the bishop's keeping diocesan affairs in his own hands that the only known papal letter addressed to Humbaud is a confirmation, at the bishop's request, of episcopal authority,

---

39. *Gesta*, p. 408. This Pseudo-Isidorian decretal was cited again at the First Lateran Council as a "sanction of the blessed pope Stephen." Mansi 1:892; Hefele–Leclercq, *Histoire des conciles*, 5, 1:633.

40. *Gesta*, pp. 404–08. The chapels of older Burgundian castles, like Varzy and Cosne, had usually obtained the status of a parish church by the end of the eleventh century: Jean Richard, "Châteaux, châtelains, et vassaux en Bourgogne aux XIe et XIIe siècles," *Cahiers de civilisation médiévale* 3 (1960), 436.

41. *Gesta*, p. 409: ". . . ne deducus fieret aecclesie."

a letter copied verbatim into the middle of the section on diocesan administration in the biography. In it, Paschal II threatened excommunication of anyone, layman or cleric, who tried to remove any of the churches of the diocese from Humbaud's obedience or tried to take away any episcopal possessions. Special emphasis was given to the bishop's personal control over episcopal property, which was alleged to have been given in perpetuity to all succeeding bishops by Saint Germain, bishop of Auxerre in the fifth century.[42]

In his emphasis on Humbaud's achievements, the biographer did not mention the wider movement of church reform taking place throughout France at that time. In a number of sees besides Auxerre, the late eleventh century saw a bishop elected canonically, without successful influence from the local nobility, for the first time in many years. Ecclesiastical reformers all over France described the reformed monastic or canonical life of common property under a strict rule as the "apostolic" life, identifying it with that led by the apostles in the earliest church.[43] The reform movement was to a large extent fueled by councils, often held by the pope. Yet the biographer mentioned no other sees, gave regularity rather than the restored apostolic life as the goal of Humbaud's reform, and mentioned no councils other than the synod Humbaud held himself and (very briefly) the council at Nîmes. He described the pope primarily as someone whom Humbaud found useful in carrying out his projects: consecrating Humbaud, deposing the abbot of St.-Germain at the bishop's request, and confirming his control over the local churches.

Surviving documents indicate, however, that Humbaud was a frequent participant in councils held outside the diocese. He was probably present at the Council of Clermont in November of 1095. Besides inspiring the First Crusade, this council promulgated a series of reforming decrees aimed at ending both clerical abuses and lay control of ecclesiastical property. Contemporary accounts indicate that all the suffragan bishops of the province of Sens were present; Humbaud, who had been consecrated by Urban II in Milan in the spring of that year, doubtless returned to France with

---

42. Ibid., pp. 406–07. Saint Germain, after whom the abbey was named, was popularly believed since the ninth century to have been a rich heir who bequeathed his patrimony, consisting of much of the land of the diocese, to those who succeeded him as bishop of Auxerre: Joachim Wollash, "Das Patrimonium Beati Germani in Auxerre," in *Studien und Arbeiten zur Geschichte des grossfränkischen und frühdeutschen Adels*, ed. Gerd Tellenbach (Breisgau, 1957), pp. 221–24.

43. M.-D. Chenu, *La théologie au douzième siècle* (Paris, 1957), pp. 227–28. Glenn Olsen, "The Idea of the *Ecclesia Primitiva* in the Writings of the Twelfth-Century Canonists," *Traditio* 25 (1969), 64–65. M.-H. Vicaire, *The Apostolic Life*, trans. William E. DeNaple (Chicago, 1966), p. 21.

the pope.[44] Besides his attendance at the Council of Nîmes mentioned above, Humbaud was also definitely present at the 1098 Council of Etampes, called to settle the disputed election of Nevers; the 1100 Council of Asne, which was primarily concerned with the Crusade; the 1104 Council of Paris, at which the French bishops agreed to absolve King Philip I from the excommunication laid on him for his elopement with Bertha of Anjou; and the 1108 Council of Fleury-sur-Loire, called to commemorate the translation of the relics of St. Benedict.[45] In addition, Humbaud attended a number of other ceremonies, many of which involved ecclesiastical reform. These included the gift by Count William I of Nevers to Cluny of the monastery of St.-Etienne of Nevers, which he had rebuilt; the papal dedication of the new edifice of the church of La Charité in 1107; the consecration of King Louis VI in 1108; and the royal foundation of the abbey of St.-Victor, outside Paris, in 1113.[46] The councils and ceremonies which the biographer did not include primarily stressed the ending of scandalous abuses within the church or the orderly establishment of reformed houses and practices, the same issues which in the biographer's view dominated Humbaud's diocesan administration. Thus, although the biographer described Humbaud's achievements as if they were unique, the bishop that emerges from the biography as well as the documents is one whose devotion to reform made him an outstanding example of the type of bishop who was bringing the results of the Gregorian Reform to the local level in many French sees.

Humbaud's biographer called him a bishop "praiseworthy in all things" (*per cuncta laudabilis*). He did so many admirable works for his church that he "deserved the praise of all good men."[47] His character and his virtue were for the most part evidenced in his successful restoration of regularity to the diocese.

Spirituality and Hospitality

The biographer devoted several sentences at the beginning of his work (part of his description of Humbaud's family background and election) and a short (300-word) passage at the end to a description of the bishop's

44. Mansi 20:816–19. Hefele-Leclercq, *Histoire des conciles*, 5, 1:398.
45. Ivo of Chartres, Letter 79, PL 162:100–01. Hugh of Flavigny. *Chronicon Virdunensis*, RHGF 13:624. Lambert of Arras, Letter 147, RHGF 15:197. Clarius of Sens, *Chronicon Sancti-Petri-Vivi Senonensis,* ed. L.-M. Duru, *Bibliothèque historique de l'Yonne* 2 (Auxerre, 1863), 518.
46. *Gallia Christiana* 12:332–36, no. 43. *Dedicatio ecclesiae B. Mariae de Caritate,* RGHF 14:120–21. Suger, *Vita Ludovici Grossi Regis* 14, ed. Henri Waquet (Paris, 1929), p. 86. *Gallia Christiana* 7:46–48, no. 55.
47. *Gesta*, p. 408.

personal virtues. He described him as harmless and wise (again, the dove and the serpent), chaste and temperate, patient but vigorous, cheerful and affable.[48] This list seems to have been inspired in part by Titus 1.7-8, and it was scarcely developed beyond a simple list. The biographer indicated that Humbaud gave a number of poor men food and clothing during Lent, while himself abstaining from meat and almost entirely from wine at all times, in order to combat the "desires of the flesh."[49] But the only virtue to which the biographer gave any emphasis was hospitality. He described Humbaud as believing that a "bishop who does not receive everyone is discourteous," echoing the words of Isidore of Seville, who said that a bishop was required to be even more hospitable than other Christians.[50] Humbaud did indeed welcome "everyone." As well as giving hospitality to pilgrims, the poor, and other churchmen, Humbaud also welcomed secular nobles. His biographer said that, though his greatest affection was reserved for clerics, he always loved to have a crowd of knights and noblemen around him.[51]

This warlike bishop was, naturally enough, not described as humble. Humility, which was stressed as a necessary episcopal virtue by Gregory the Great and the biographer of Humbaud's successor, was mentioned only once: the biographer said that the bishop overcame the local laymen with "humility and patience" when he paid them to end depredations to the church, but the context of the term scarcely conveys the meekness and modesty of the Christian virtue.[52] Humbaud's biographer was not attempting to describe a saint but rather an effective reformer.[53] It may be that he spent little space on Humbaud's personal spirituality because he could take for granted the virtues of a reforming bishop. He stressed Humbaud's hospitality, but for the most part he showed that Humbaud was a "praise-worthy" bishop by describing his administrative reforms, not his spirituality.

48. Ibid., pp. 402, 408: ". . . simplicitate et prudentia, castitate ac temperantia, ceterisque virtutum floribus pollens." "Erat enim sagacis ingenii, prudens eloquio, providus in consilio, paciencia lenis, vultu alacris, incessu et habitu jocundus, erga omnes benigne affabilis."
49. Ibid., p. 409: ". . . illicitis siquidem motibus carnis."
50. Ibid. Isidore of Seville, *De ecclesiasticis officiis* 2.5, PL 83:780-86: "Episcopus, nisi omnes receperit, inhumanus est."
51. *Gesta*, p. 409: ". . . diligebat militum atque nobilium contubernia."
52. Ibid.: "Mira ejus paciencia atque humilitatis gratis discordantes animos concordabat, et ut pax fieret firmior et quies, inquietanti dande de suo sepenumero propinabat."
53. The Bollandists make Humbaud a saint, although they could find no record of any twelfth-century cult—nor can I. Urban VIII declared him a saint in the seventeenth century, on the basis of a sixteenth-century cult; AASS Oct. 8:996-1007.

Conclusions

The biographer described a bishop of tremendous vigor. He gave Humbaud all the credit for restoring regularity to the religious houses of the diocese, wresting episcopal property from usurpers, and rebuilding parts of the dilapidated cathedral. The biographer drew no explicit contrast between Humbaud and his predecessor Robert, in fact referring to Robert as a man of "glorious and honorable" character (*gloriosus decusque*),[54] but the contrast was plain between a bishop who allowed a scandalous abbot to head St.-Germain, the local nobility to take episcopal property for their own use, and the cathedral roof to decay during the fifteen years he held office, and a bishop who spent twenty years rectifying these problems. Humbaud remained vigorous until well past seventy, when, according to the biographer, he went on a pilgrimage to Jerusalem, both for "remission of his sins" and for the purpose of bringing back ornaments and relics for his church. The bishop and the ornaments were lost together at sea on the return journey.[55]

The biographer, perhaps reflecting the bias of a cathedral canon, put most of the emphasis in his account of this vigorous bishop's accomplishments on the affairs of the cathedral. He gave much more space to Humbaud's acquisition of episcopal land and the gifts he made to his chapter and the cathedral edifice than he did to Humbaud's reform of local houses. Even when describing the reform of St.-Germain and the foundation of Pontigny, he said that St.-Germain was submitted to the bishop's rule and that Pontigny was founded on land given by a cathedral canon; these details of how the churches were linked to the cathedral took precedence over their reformed inner life.

In stressing the central role of the bishop and his chapter in diocesan affairs, the biographer also failed to indicate that Humbaud had the help of the pope in many of his successful reforms and that he often took part in ecclesiastical synods held outside the diocese. But to some extent this emphasis on the bishop's leading role in the restoration of regularity is valid. The papal reformers of the eleventh and early twelfth centuries gave local bishops the responsibiliṭy for implementing the reforms that their councils decreed. Papal reorganization of the hierarchical structure did not reach directly into the local units of the church until well into the twelfth century. Bishops no longer had the freedom to make liturgical innovations

54. *Gesta*, pp. 402, 408.
55. Ibid., p. 409: ". . . pro salvatoris amore et peccatorum suorum remissione, Jherosolimitanum prosecutus est iter . . . dum rediret et ecclesiae suae ornamenta plurima deferret. . . ."

and create and interpret ecclesiastical law, as they had fifty years earlier, but in local ecclesiastical affairs, the bishop himself, not the pope, archbishop, or king, made most of the decisions.[56]

For the biographer, an excellent bishop and an excellent administrator were essentially the same. Only in a few places did he hint that Humbaud's success was not complete. He said that the bishop would have made more improvements to the cathedral and made more gifts to the chapter if it were not for certain laymen. He also indicated that on occasion the bishop "humbly" made payments to laymen when concluding a peace with them. In the context of his remarks about the bishop's hospitable welcome of the knights he loved to have around him, it is clear that the biographer considered Humbaud's only failures to have come from an excess of hospitality, even though hospitality was the only virtue he emphasized. He saw a bishop's excellence as residing not so much in his spirituality as in his administrative accomplishments.

It was not however always necessary for a bishop of Auxerre to be a great administrator in order to be admired by his biographer. The biographer of Humbaud's successor, describing a very different sort of man, reversed the priorities of Humbaud's biographer and put most of his emphasis on his subject's spiritual qualities.

56. Lemarignier, Gaudemet, and Mollat, *Institutions ecclésiastiques*, p. 111. Southern, *Western Society and the Church*, p. 188.

II

HUGH OF MONTAIGU
AND MONASTIC WITHDRAWAL

The description of the pontificate of Hugh of Montaigu (1115-1136) given by his anonymous biographer is in large part a description of his virtues, chief among them humility, a virtue scarcely mentioned by Humbaud's biographer. The biographer regarded humility as a monastic quality that was evident in Hugh's love of poverty and simplicity, his deference to others in the ecclesiastical hierarchy, and his encouragement of the foundation of new monasteries. After a description of Hugh's early years and his election to the see of Auxerre, the biographer began his description of the bishop's accomplishments with the statement, "The following will show with what purity of soul and with what humility he lived as bishop."[1]

Hugh's origins were not humble in any social or economic sense; his relatives included outstanding ecclesiastical and secular leaders. His father was Dalmace, lord of the castle of Montaigu, near Cluny. His aunt Helias had married Robert I, duke of Burgundy. His uncle Hugh was abbot of Cluny (1049-1109). One cousin, Rainald, was abbot of Vézelay (1106-1125) and archbishop of Lyon (1125-1128); another, Gervais, succeeded Hugh as abbot of St.-Germain of Auxerre when Hugh was elected bishop. Hugh of Montaigu had been made a monk at Cluny under his uncle and namesake, became abbot of St.-Germain in 1100 when Humbaud reformed that house, and was elected bishop of Auxerre in 1115.

As in 1092, the election sparked a controversy among the cathedral canons. According to Hugh's biographer, some of the canons quickly elected Hugh when news of Humbaud's death reached Auxerre. Others, however, led by Humbaud's nephew Ulger, whom Humbaud had made provost and who now wanted to become bishop himself, resisted Hugh's election and gained the support of King Louis VI, who refused Hugh the temporal regalia of his office. At the beginning of the century, a rough agreement on the investiture of French bishops had been worked out between Louis's father Philip I and the pope, according to which a newly elected bishop would have to be invested with the regalia by the king

---

1. *Gesta*, p. 411: "Denique in quanta animi puritate et quam humilis in episcopatu suo vixerit . . . subsequens littera declarabit."

before he could take up the administration of the diocese.[2] Hugh, unable to assume his duties, appealed to Pope Paschal II.

This was the first episcopal election at Auxerre ever appealed to the Roman curia. Ulger may have expected the pope's favor, since Paschal had taken him and his possessions under the protection of the apostolic see when he became provost (see Chapter I). But the pope decided in favor of Hugh and personally consecrated him. Hugh's biographer, describing the election as taking place with the canonical approval of "clergy and people," recorded that the people of Auxerre gave Hugh a formal acclamation on his return from Rome, that the count of Nevers, who had been captured in battle, sent word from prison of his approval, and that the king, facing a bishop consecrated by the pope himself, was quickly "pacified."[3]

Monastic Humility

Immediately after this account of Hugh's election, the biographer began his description of the bishop's "purity of soul" and "humility." He made very little distinction between virtues proper for a monk and those proper for a bishop. He always described Hugh's spirituality in monastic terms; indeed he described Hugh's promotion first to abbot and then to bishop as God's reward for the humility he displayed as a monk.[4] This humility, said the biographer, together with his habit of constantly repeating the Ave Maria, were clear signs that the bishop had received saving grace. He repeatedly called Hugh a *sanctus vir* throughout his work. On the basis of this enthusiastic description, Pope Urban VIII declared in the seventeenth century that Hugh had long been recognized as a saint, but there is little evidence of a twelfth-century cult.[5]

The biographer described Hugh as frequently deferring to others in obedience to Jesus' command to the apostles, "He that is greatest among you, let him be as the younger, and he that is chief, as he that doth serve" (Luke 22.26). He also said that Hugh, who had lived most of his life in a monastery before his election to the see of Auxerre, expressed humility in withdrawal to the cloister, always remembering the words of Jerome, a "teacher of monks": "To me a town is a prison and solitude a paradise. If you wish to be what you call *monachus*, that is, one alone, what are you doing in the city?"[6] Although Hugh did not completely abandon diocesan

---

2. Robert L. Benson, *The Bishop-Elect* (Princeton, 1968), pp. 229–35, 313.

3. *Gesta*, pp. 410–11.

4. Ibid.: "Dominus omnipotens, qui humilia respecit in coelo et in terra, humilitatem hujus respiciens multis profuturam eum in claustro diu manere non permisit."

5. Ibid., p. 411. AASS Aug. 2:550–60.

6. *Gesta*, p. 411. He is paraphrasing Jerome's letter 125, PL 22:1076–77.

administration in search of humility, the biographer indicated that he frequently withdrew from Auxerre and the cares of his office to retreat to La Charité, a Cluniac house in the southwest corner of the diocese, or more often to the new Cistercian house of Clairvaux.

The biographer made some distinction between the Cluniac and the Cistercian orders of monks, calling each by its name, whereas Humbaud's biographer had called both of them "orders of monks living under the Rule of St. Benedict." Yet he did not portray Hugh as being aware of the conflict between the ideals of the two orders that became explicit in the early 1120s in the letters between Peter the Venerable, abbot of Cluny, and Bernard of Clairvaux. Rather, he portrayed a man who adopted the spiritual goals of both orders during his career, never formally renouncing either.

The biographer first described Hugh as living in humble patience and deference to his elders at Cluny, "as a monk should." This patience and obedience meant, in Cluniac spirituality, renunciation of self-will and attainment of the highest rung of the ladder of humility set out in the Benedictine Rule.[7] Cluny, which had been one of the most influential centers of monastic life in the eleventh century, lost much of its ascendancy in the early twelfth century to the new religious orders, especially the order of Cîteaux. The Cistercian order began its period of growth when Bernard joined the monastery, three years before Hugh became bishop of Auxerre. The biographer, having already shown Hugh as living the ideal of Cluniac humility, went on to describe him as living the Cistercian ideal as well. The Cistercians had deliberately set out to follow Benedict's Rule more closely than did the existing monastic orders. They performed heavy manual labor, which the Cluniacs had given up in favor of a prolonged liturgy. They enforced the Benedictine prescription of a long probationary noviciate, which the Cluniacs had greatly reduced. Most significantly in their own eyes, the Cistercians sought a life of asceticism and austerity, consciously distinct from Cluny's luxury and extensive possessions. To the Cluniac definition of humility as patience and obedience, the Cistercians added poverty, simplicity, and withdrawal from the cares and the honors

---

7. *Gesta*, p. 410: "Semper sine querela, humilis et obediens suis majoribus, sicut decet monachum, permansit." For the ladder of humility, see St. Benedict, *Regula* 7, ed. Adalbert de Vogüé and Jean Neufville, *La règle de Saint Benoît*, Sources chrétiennes 181 (Paris, 1971-72), 1:472-91. Barbara H. Rosenwein and Lester K. Little, "Social Meaning in the Monastic and Mendicant Spiritualities," *Past and Present* 63 (1974), 5-6. Etienne Gilson, *The Mystical Theology of Saint Bernard*, trans. A. H. C. Downes (New York, 1940), p. 29. For an example of Cluniac spirituality with its emphasis on prayer and contemplation rather than labor, see Jean Leclercq, *La spiritualité de Pierre de Celle* (Paris, 1946), pp. 139-40.

of the world.[8] Hugh's biographer said that he embraced the "joyful and voluntary poverty" (*leta et voluntaria paupertas*) of this new order and often retreated to Clairvaux to be with Bernard, the best-known member of the Cistercian order, who drew many to Christ through "his doctrine and the example of his way of life."[9]

At Clairvaux, Hugh's biographer recorded approvingly, Hugh wished to be treated like one of the brothers, being called "monk" rather than "bishop." He worked in the abbey's fields, side-by-side with Bernard and the brothers, expecting, in his biographer's words, "great spiritual reward" from association with them in their labors. Thus he continued to demonstrate the humble deference he had earlier displayed as a Cluniac monk. One of the spiritual rewards which the biographer described Hugh as receiving was the grace to help perform a miracle. Once, while Hugh was helping harvest wheat, a storm came up, threatening the crop. Bernard, according to the biographer, remembered that "All things are possible to him that believeth" (Mark 9.22) and asked Hugh to pray that the storm recede; Hugh was too humble to pray until Bernard agreed to join him, at which time the storm clouds moved off quickly. The "sainted harvesters" (*sancti messores*) were able to finishing gathering the crop easily.[10] In describing this miracle, which I have not found among any accounts of the miracles of Bernard, the biographer indicated his understanding of the holiness of those who followed the Cistercian life. Hugh's participation in the miracle certainly suggests the biographer's belief that it was suitable for a bishop to leave his other affairs for the monastic life whenever possible. If the account of Hugh's working next to Bernard is authentic, the bishop's retreats to Clairvaux probably began in the first years of his pontificate, indicating the immediate attraction for him of the Cistercian order; Clairvaux had been founded the same year he became bishop, and Bernard only worked in the fields at Clairvaux for the first few years, because he soon became too weak to participate in manual labor.[11]

---

8. David Knowles, "Cistercians and Cluniacs: The Controversy Between St. Bernard and Peter the Venerable," *The Historian and Character and Other Essays* (Cambridge, Eng., 1963), pp. 50–75. François Vanderbrouke, *La morale monastique du XIe au XVIe siècle* (Louvain, 1966), pp. 120–21. Gilson, *Mystical Theology*, pp. 68–74. The anonymous author of the mid-twelfth-century *Libellus de diversis ordinibus et professionibus qui sunt in aecclesia* called the Cluniacs monks who live near men and the Cistercians monks who live far from men: ed. Giles Constable and B. Smith (Oxford, 1972), pp. 18, 44.

9. *Gesta*, pp. 411, 414: ". . . domnus Bernardus venerabilis, magni nominis et meriti abbas cujus vita et doctrina in universali aecclesia celebriter divulgata multo secum traxit ad Christum."

10. Ibid., pp. 411–12, 414–15.

11. David Knowles, "Saint Bernard of Clairvaux," *The Historian and Character*, p. 37.

Hugh's biographer wrote his description of a bishop who found grace in monastic humility and withdrawal at a time when many ecclesiastical authors stressed the need for such a way of life in order to make spiritual progress. Peter Damian (1007–1072) had said that true aspiration to God could only be expressed in a simple life, withdrawn from the world. Authors of the early twelfth century continued his emphasis on simplicity and asceticism as the way to salvation. This simple life was often called the *vita apostolica*, the way of life believed to have been practiced in the earliest church. Though Hugh's biographer did not use the term (and indeed I have found it in no text from the Auxerrois), he expressed a similar concept in saying that Hugh obeyed the commands of humility that Jesus gave his apostles. Emphasis on the *vita apostolica* was found both in houses of reformed monks and houses of canons regular and, increasingly as the twelfth century progressed, in groups of wandering and preaching *pauperes Christi*. All these groups grew very rapidly at the beginning of the twelfth century; the life of poverty and humility, in whatever context it was expressed, appealed strongly to men from all ranks of the clergy and also to many laymen.[12]

A number of French bishops besides Hugh of Montaigu felt the attraction of finding salvation through the monastic life, especially in the new reformed houses, Chartreuse and the houses of the Cistercian order. The bishop of Châlons-sur-Marne left his see for an entire year to live at Clairvaux. Geoffrey of Amiens abandoned his see for Chartreuse in 1114, although he was summoned back by a regional council within the year. Hugh of Grenoble (1080–1132) was described by his biographer as frequently joining St. Bruno and the brothers at Chartreuse for a period of humility and fervent contemplation. Bishops Anselm of Canterbury (1093–1109), Ivo of Chartres (1090–1115), Norbert of Magdeburg (1126–1134), and Odo of Cambrai (1105–1113) had all been monks, as bishops they all continued to observe monastic regulations on food and dress, and after their deaths they were all commemorated as saints. In every case, the biographers of these bishops stressed their humility.[13]

12. Vandenbrouke, *La morale monastique*, pp. 39–40. Herbert Grundmann, *Religiöse Bewegungen im Mittelalter,* 2nd ed. (Hildesheim, 1961), p. 506. Jean Leclercq, François Vandenbrouke, and Louis Bouyer, *La spiritualité du moyen âge,* Histoire de la spiritualité chrétienne 3 (Paris, 1961), pp. 161–62. For the appeal of the *vita apostolica,* see also Guibert de Nogent, *De vita sua* 1.11, ed. Georges Bourgin (Paris, 1907), pp. 30–36.

13. For the bishop of Châlons, see the *Vita prima Sancti Bernardi* 1.7, PL 185:246. For Geoffrey of Amiens, see Guibert de Nogent, *De vita sua* 3.14, ed. Bourgin, pp. 200–01. For Hugh of Grenoble, see Guigo of Chartreuse, *Vita Sancti Hugonis episcopi Gratianopolitani,* AASS April 1:37–46. For Anselm, see Eadmer, *Vita Sancti Anselmi archiepiscopi Cantuariensis,* ed. R. W. Southern (London, 1962).

Although Bernard of Clairvaux, the great spokesman of Cistercian ideals, discouraged bishops from abandoning their sees for the cloister, he urged them to practice virtues very like the virtues characteristic of the reformed monks of the early twelfth century. In a treatise on the life a bishop should lead, the *Tractatus de moribus et officio episcoporum*, which grew from a letter he wrote to Archbishop Henry of Sens in 1127/8, he urged bishops to adopt humility, chastity, and charity.[14] There are a number of parallels between this *Tractatus* and the biography of Hugh of Montaigu. Though Hugh's biographer did not dwell on *castitas* and *caritas*, so important in Bernard's discussion, like Bernard he emphasized the importance of *humilitas*, of poverty and withdrawal from the praises and splendor of the world. Bernard and the biographer even used some of the same biblical references (such as Luke 22.26, cited above). Thus the cathedral canon who wrote Hugh's biography, though certainly not paraphrasing the *Tractatus*, expressed a concept of the virtues proper for a bishop in monastic terms, terms close to those used by one of the great monastic figures of his time.

Even when discussing those of Hugh's virtues which were not specific to monasticism, he tended to give them a monastic cast. He frequently mentioned Hugh's concern for the purity of his conscience (*puritas conscientiae*), a concern Bernard also found necessary in a bishop.[15] The biographer related that Hugh immediately returned a gift of money his church badly needed when he discovered that it came from a man to whom he had given an ecclesiastical benefice, out of fear that in accepting it he might "pollute" his conscience (*ne conscientia mea polluatur*). He was equally scrupulous in returning the money he had been given by the local churches for a projected trip to Rome after he decided not to go. He was concerned not only about the impurity of accepting a gift that smacked of simony or which he could not use as intended, but also about having too many possessions of his own; several times when he fell sick, his biographer stated, he gave away all the moveable goods he possessed, including even his silver spoons, afraid that if he retained anything it would

---

Ivo of Chartres has no contemporary *vita*; a modern survey of his life and work is found in Rolf Sprandel, *Ivo von Chartres und seine Stellung in der Kirchengeschichte* (Stuttgart, 1962). For Norbert of Magdeburg, see the *Vita Norberti archiepiscopi Magdeburgensis*, MGH SS 12:670-706. For Odo of Cambrai, see Amand of Castello, *Vita Beati Odoni episcopi Cameracensis*, AASS June 4:761-73.

14. Bernard of Clairvaux, *Opera*, ed. Jean Leclercq and Henri Rochais, 7 (Rome, 1974), 100-31.

15. Ibid., pp. 117-21.

"offend the purity of his conscience."[16] The biographer's description of Hugh's insistence on poverty for the good of his soul suggests the concept expressed by contemporary Cistercian authors, who saw poverty as a necessary element of rededication to God, a necessary element in the humility that restores the image of God in man.[17]

Hugh's biographer gave the bulk of his attention to this treatment of his subject's virtues, virtues which in the biographer's eyes made it clear that Hugh had received saving grace, virtues which were expressed in a monastic way of life that included both Cluniac and Cistercian elements. Yet in spite of Hugh's penchant for a withdrawn life, he never left his diocese to the administration of the chapter for long. The biographer showed him as able to reconcile in practice the choice, faced by many bishops at the beginning of the twelfth century, between a personal quest for holiness and effective diocesan administration.

Care for the Diocese

The biographer considered the roles of the bishop as holy man and as diocesan administrator to be closely linked; his saintly bishop was one who adopted the monastic virtues in his own life and encouraged the other ecclesiastics of his diocese to do likewise. "As a good master should, he began to act and to teach, demonstrating by example what he taught" (cf. Acts 1.1). The good master, who was compared to Christ, acted by founding new monastic houses and taught the value of the reformed monastic life by following it himself.

In recounting Hugh's devotion to the Cistercian order and his frequent withdrawals to the cloister, the biographer described his generosity to the Cistercian house of Pontigny, which had been founded the year before his consecration, and to the three Cistercian houses he himself founded in the diocese, at Reigny, Bouras, and Les Roches. The house at Reigny was established by the brothers of Fontemois, the house to which Humbaud had given a rule around 1105 (see Chapter I); in 1128, Fontemois adopted a Cistercian rule, and a few years later the brothers moved their house several miles to Reigny. Bouras and Les Roches were founded as daughter houses of Pontigny in 1119 and 1136.[18]

16. *Gesta*, pp. 412–14: ". . . ut nichil sibi retineret, quod conscientie sue puritatem offendere posset."
17. Leclercq, Vandenbrouke, and Bouyer, *La spiritualité du moyen âge*, p. 242. Patrick Ryan, "The Witness of William of St.-Thierry to the Spirit and Aims of the Early Cistercians," in *The Cistercian Spirit: A Symposium in Memory of Thomas Merton*, ed. M. Basil Pennington (Spencer, Mass., 1970), pp. 224–53.
18. *Gesta*, p. 411. For Reigny, see also Quantin 1.175, 185, pp. 299–300, 312–13.

Hugh's biographer mentioned only the foundation of Cistercian houses, but other sources reveal additional foundations or restorations of monasteries by Hugh. He was instrumental in establishing regular nuns of the order of Jully at Crisenon, which had been made a priory of Molesme under Humbaud but which was turned over to the nuns by the brothers of Molesme sometime before 1134. He agreed to the rebuilding by one of the cathedral canons of the long-abandoned monastery of St.-Marien in 1126; this house became a house of Premonstratensian canons under Hugh's immediate successor, and the late-twelfth-century chronicler Robert of St.-Marien was to remember Hugh as a man of "great vision" for this restoration. Hugh also established Augustinian canons regular at the priory of St.-Amatre, just southwest of Auxerre, and endowed them with several parish churches and tithes.[19] Both Hugh's biography and his existing charters indicated that he was very generous both to the houses he helped found and to the ones already in the diocese when he took office. To the older established houses of St.-Germain, St.-Julien, and St.-Pierre, according to his charters, he gave the churches and tithes he received from lay hands. He obtained a bull from Calixtus II in 1120 confirming his right to distribute these churches as he saw best.[20]

The biographer, a cathedral canon, also recorded that the bishop was generous to the chapter of Auxerre and treated the canons with fatherly concern. His chief endeavor to improve their welfare was to suppress the office of chapter provost. Provost Ulger, according to the biographer, had caused a bitter quarrel between himself and the rest of the canons, but Hugh settled the quarrel, in a concern for peace which the biographer likened to that of St. Martin, and had the pope confirm the agreement he reached: "Mark the perfect man . . . for the end of that man is peace" (Psalm 37.37).[21] As neither the episcopal nor the papal charter describing the agreement still exists, the object of the dispute is not known, but Ulger, who had already caused the controversy over Hugh's election, seems to have considered his office a position from which to try to gain more power. When Ulger died, sometime after 1130,[22] Hugh did not appoint a new provost but instead gave the revenues from the office's prebend to the chapter as a whole, thinking, in his biographer's words, that "nothing could be more useful to the common good." Thus, while assuring that there could be no further quarrels involving the provost, Hugh gave his

19. For Crisenon, see Quantin 1.176, pp. 301–02. For St.-Marien, see Robert of St.-Marien, pp. 231–32. For St.-Amatre, see Quantin 1.164, pp. 284–86.
20. Quantin 1.134, 135, 138, 163, pp. 250–52, 256, 283–84.
21. Gesta, p. 415.
22. When he last appeared in a dated charter: Quantin 1.163, p. 283.

canons, whose income came from individual prebends, the income from the provostry to be shared in common, in the monastic fashion. The biographer did not explain who assumed the duties of the provost's office and administered the chapter's temporal goods; presumably it was some of the other cathedral dignitaries. Though Hugh had the pope confirm his gift of the provostry to his chapter, the biographer commented with disapproval that the donation was not observed by his successor.[23] As well as suppressing the office of provost, Hugh also suppressed the office of archdeacon, probably around 1123, when Archdeacon Roger disappears from the records. Though in this case Hugh kept the revenues from the office in his own hands rather than distributing them to the chapter as a whole, the biographer was at pains to point out that he did not act out of greed but, again, out of a fatherly concern for the canons' welfare: the revenues were insufficient for the support of the archdeacon, he said, and the priest who tried to carry out the duties of the office on such a small stipend would be seriously burdened.[24] The office of the archdeacon, however, like the office of the provost, was filled again under Hugh's successor.[25]

Hugh had introduced some monastic elements into his chapter when he gave the canons the provostry's revenues to be shared in common rather than to be divided among the canons' separate prebends. His documents indicated another occasion when an episcopal gift had monastic overtones. He promised the canons four parish churches and the tithes from a fifth, to hold as long as they would eat together in a common refectory, on the monastic model, each year during Lent. This change was scarcely radical, but it did indicate the value Hugh put on common life, which was a distinguishing feature of reformed religious houses.[26]

Hugh redistributed ecclesiastical property for the benefit of the new reformed houses of the diocese and the cathedral canons, but he was also very generous with his own goods. The biographer recorded that in a year when the grape harvest was disastrously meager the bishop distributed wine from his own cellars to Crisenon, the four Cistercian houses, and the Cluniac house of La Charité to which he sometimes withdrew from the pressures of the city. Refusing to be stingy, he even gave the nuns of Crisenon some of his own stock of wine from the renowned vineyards of Migraine, over the objections of his cellarer, who urged him to remember

23. *Gesta,* p. 416.
24. Ibid., p. 412: ". . . non propter avaritiam, sed ne sacerdotes gravarentur, sciens archidiaconatus redditus paucissimos esse."
25. Quantin 1.209, pp. 348–49.
26. Ibid., 1.182, pp. 309–10.

45

the high price of Migraine wine and to give the nuns something of lesser value. Hugh was so determined that the nuns should have this gift that when their *dispensator* sold the Migraine wine and bought a cheaper wine instead, Hugh insisted he buy it back and even gave him the amount he would have made on the sale to be sure he would not be tempted to sell it again. When he was being generous, Hugh showed a sharpness and firmness that the biographer did not normally attribute to him. "Do you not know that the word of a bishop should never be ignored?" Hugh is recorded as saying to his cautious cellarer.[27] The biographer dwelt on this incident at some length, saying that it demonstrated the bishop's generosity, his love for the local houses, and his belief that one should not "take heed of those things which are of God" (Matt. 16.23).[28]

Hugh's determined generosity to the nuns of Crisenon is indicative of a belief that he knew what was best for the churches of his diocese even when they did not. His documents indicate similarly that, in spite of his frequent retreats from the city, he continued to be the chief authority in the administration of his diocese. Although the chapter sometimes handled in his absence such affairs as a gift to a local monastery, the canons had him confirm their decision on his return.[29] Hugh personally settled the only dispute involving a church in the diocese that is known to have occurred during his episcopate; when St.-Germain and the count of Nevers quarreled violently over the administration of justice to men living next to the abbey church, Hugh arranged a compromise that satisfied both the count and his own cousin Gervais, abbot of St.-Germain.[30]

Apparently the count and the king played no direct part in the affairs of the diocese of Auxerre, other than their partisan interest in Hugh's election, even though the king was quite involved in the affairs of Sens, the archbishopric of the ecclesiastical province that included Paris.[31] The only

---

27. *Gesta*, pp. 413–14. The vineyards of Migraine, located a short distance northwest of Auxerre, were famous for the quality of their wine as early as the sixth century and were still highly regarded in the eighteenth. The vines were almost completely destroyed during the phylloxera plague of the nineteenth century.

28. The biographer apparently used this passage to indicate that Hugh was not stingy with what God had given him, although in the biblical passage Peter is rebuked because he does not take heed of the (spiritual) things of God.

29. See for example the gift from the treasurer of the chapter to Pontigny in 1120 (Quantin 1.129, pp. 243–44), and the provost's enumeration of Molesme's dependent churches in the diocese (Quantin 1.146, pp. 264–65). In both cases, the bishop later confirmed.

30. *De Gestibus Abbatum S. Germani Autissiodorensis*, ed. Philippe Labbe, *Novae bibliothecae manuscriptorum librorum*, 1 (Paris, 1657), 576.

31. The king defended Sens's primacy in 1121 against the pope's attempts to make Lyon the primatial see of France, even though the city of Lyon lay within the boundaries of the empire: Quantin 1.131, pp. 245–47.

charters which the archbishop of Sens is known to have issued to any house of Auxerre during Hugh's pontificate were addressed to Pontigny, a house which lay on the border of the diocese of Sens and Auxerre with property in both.[32] None of Hugh's decisions were appealed over his head to the pope. The pope's letters concerning the diocesan affairs of Auxerre are for the most part confirmations, at Hugh's request, of something the bishop had already done;[33] the biographer only mentioned the pope twice, once as settling Hugh's election and once as confirming an episcopal decision.

All over France at this time bishops were being confirmed in their diocesan authority. The First Lateran Council, held by Calixtus II in 1123, issued a number of canons strengthening the bishop's position. (As no list of participants survives, it is impossible to say whether Hugh attended.) At this council, the bishop was declared to have final *judicio* and *potestas* over all ecclesiastical goods and to be alone responsible for the direction of the care of souls and visitations of churches in his diocese. Throughout the first several decades of the twelfth century, although popes wrote to local churches more frequently than they had in the eleventh century, they rarely took overt action beyond confirming possessions or granting monasteries such requested honors and benefices as the use of miters or perhaps freedom from episcopal jurisdiction.[34]

Episcopal autonomy would not, however, persist long after the early years of the twelfth century. The pope began to play a judicial role in many dioceses, especially after the accession of Innocent II in 1130. At Auxerre, the pope himself settled Hugh's disputed election, though Humbaud's election had been settled by the canons before his trip to Rome for confirmation. Innocent II acted as judge in a local dispute in 1139, when he arbitrated a case involving Hugh and determined that the Cistercian house of Reigny should owe obedience to the bishop of Auxerre, not the bishop of Autun, for while the original foundation of Fontemois could be

32. In 1126, the archbishop granted the monks that they need not pay him tithes for lands they cultivated directly in his diocese: Quantin 1.143, pp. 261–62. He expanded this privilege to include all their property in his diocese in 1127: ibid., 1.150, pp. 269–70.

33. Pope Innocent II made several short stays in Auxerre in 1131 during his travels through France, where he was recognized as the legitimate pope although there was a rival claimant in Rome. On one of these visits he dedicated the altar of the rebuilt house of St.-Marien and confirmed the establishment of canons regular at St.-Amatre: Quantin 1.135, pp. 251–52; Robert of St.-Marien, pp. 232–33.

34. Hefele-Leclercq, *Histoire des conciles*, 5, 1:630–44. Raymond Foreville, *Latran I, II, III et Latran IV* (Paris, 1965), p. 65. R. W. Southern, *Western Society and the Church in the Middle Ages* (Harmondsworth, Eng., 1970), pp. 113–15. No house of the Auxerrois is known to have gained exemption from episcopal jurisdiction.

construed as lying in the diocese of Autun, Reigny clearly could not. None of Humbaud's settlements had been adjudicated by the pope.[35]

But for the most part the biographer's picture of Hugh's administration seems valid: he was a bishop who could combine monastic retreat with control of diocesan affairs. Only in passing did the biographer suggest that Hugh was less than a completely successful bishop: "he was not very assiduous in some of the affairs of his church, because he sought quiet in the cloisters."[36] The biographer's hints are rather vague here. He was not faulting the bishop's relations with his chapter, for he had just described the bishop's "great care" for his church as shown in his settling the quarrel between the provost and the rest of the canons. He had also described Hugh as moved by a "spirit of prophecy" to deny admittance into the chapter of a monk at St.-Germain for fear he would divert the cathedral revenues for his own use, which happened under Hugh's successor. The biographer was not faulting the bishop's care for episcopal property within the city, for a few lines further on he described with praise the new roof and porch that Hugh added to the episcopal palace. The new roof was necessary because one of the cathedral towers had collapsed onto it in the night, so that the falling beams only narrowly missed the sleeping bishop, an escape due to the miraculous intervention of Him who neither slumbers nor sleeps but keepeth Israel (Psalm 121.4), according to the biographer, "for unless God guards a city, the watchman waketh but in vain" (Psalm 127.1).[37]

Where Hugh seems to have failed to be a completely successful administrator was in not continuing his predecessor's struggle to keep church property out of lay hands. Hugh's biographer did not mention episcopal defense of property and rights against laymen at all. The biographer of Hugh's immediate successor, however, was quite definite on this topic, stating that his subject faced a major task in recovering church property that had improperly passed into lay hands because of a "lack of justice" (*defectum justiciae*) in Hugh.[38] Hugh had been able to reconcile his choice of a monastic mode of life with some but not all of the affairs of his office: he was able to keep peace, care for the needs of local clerics with fatherly concern, and do what was best for them even when they did not recognize it as such, but he did not bring strong action against the recalcitrant laymen of the diocese.

35. Innocent II, Letter 73, PL 179:116.
36. *Gesta*, p. 415: ". . . non multum assiduus esset in ecclesia sua, ob quietem spiritus quam inveniebat inter claustrales."
37. Ibid., pp. 412, 415–16.
38. Ibid., p. 418.

Conclusions

Hugh's biographer presented him as a man of undoubted sanctity, whose inner spiritual grace was manifested in his external adoption of the monastic way of life. The biographer dwelt especially on Hugh's humility, a virtue which Humbaud's biographer had mentioned only once, but which was a central theme in the writings of monastic authors of the early twelfth century, especially Bernard, and in the biographies of many of the monastic bishops of the time. He likened him to St. Martin, the father of French monasticism, said that he obeyed Jerome on the proper life for a monk, and put special emphasis on the bishop's foundation and support of monastic houses.

This highly commendable life, however, meant that, in his biographer's eyes, Hugh was not very diligent in some episcopal duties. It was hard for a man to retreat to the cloister, emerging only to make sure the local churches were still peaceful and prosperous, and still wage a vigorous campaign against the local nobility. The contemporary monk-bishop Anselm of Canterbury was described by his biographer as finding his see's temporal affairs (*secularia negotia*) unsupportable and physically sickening.[39] It is quite possible that Hugh, who had turned from Cluny to Cîteaux, had also turned quite deliberately away from the Cluniac interest in acquiring new lands and constructing new buildings, which was quite marked in the early years of the twelfth century, in sharp contrast with early Cistercian poverty.[40] It is also probable that the amount of episcopal business which had to be attended to was quite small; diocesan administration could be carried out with an easily variable rhythm, and Humbaud had already reformed the worst abuses calling for attention in the area of temporal administration.

Except for his lack of diligence in temporal matters, everything that Hugh did was found by the biographer to be highly admirable and indicative of the bishop's sanctity. While Humbaud's biographer had recorded a series of dismal situations which the bishop vigorously rectified, Hugh's biographer described an episcopate marked by incidents in which the bishop was called on to display his virtues and his piety, usually with a biblical quotation to explain what he did. Called by Him who "giveth his beloved sleep" (Psalm 127.2), Hugh passed away quietly with the canons singing around him and was buried at St.-Germain.[41] But there are indi-

39. Eadmer, *Vita Sancti Anselmi* 2.13, ed. Southern, p. 80.
40. Georges Duby, "Le budget de l'abbaye de Cluny entre 1080 et 1155: Economie domaniale et économie monétaire," *Hommes et structures du moyen âge* (Paris, 1973), pp. 67–68.
41. *Gesta*, p. 416.

cations that, at the peaceful end of this long episcopate, there was some feeling in the cathedral chapter that a bishop should be more vigorous in temporal administration than Hugh had been. The chapter proceeded to elect, without quarrel or delay, a man whose biographer described him as a rigorous defender of ecclesiastical rights, making pointed comparisons with other bishops, especially Hugh of Montaigu.

III

HUGH OF MACON AND THE RIGOROUS PURSUIT OF JUSTICE

The anonymous biographer of Hugh of Mâcon (1136–1151) emphasized not humility but justice. The words *rigor* and *iustitia* (and often *rigor iustitiae*) appear frequently throughout the biography. He began by saying that Hugh of Mâcon was from the region of Cluny, like his predecessor and namesake, but then quickly distinguished the two by speaking of the "lack of justice" (*defectum iustitiae*) in Hugh of Montaigu which made it necessary for Hugh of Mâcon vigorously to recover lost property. The biographer greatly admired Hugh of Mâcon for his pursuit of "justice," by which he meant the defense and expansion of episcopal rights. Yet he also felt uneasy about the effects that Hugh's vigorous administration had on his personal expressions of spirituality.

The biography of Hugh is one of the shorter biographies of the twelfth-century bishops of Auxerre, less than 1100 words. Almost the entire work is an account of Hugh's greatness as evidenced through his rigorous justice and his control over all the affairs of the diocese. After a few sentences on Hugh's election and consecration, the biographer said that "He came from a family of great men, but in his greatheartedness (*animi magnanimitatem*) he conferred more greatness on his family than they on him."[1] The rest of the biography described his rigor against those who attacked the church (the attacks are described very vaguely), a few improvements to the episcopal palace and gifts to the cathedral chapter, and his measures to retain control over diocesan churches. These topics were not grouped in any particular order, but in almost every description of an episcopal action the biographer stated that Hugh was following the prescript of the Bible or the example of one of the Fathers.

This pursuer of justice is said by several sources to have come from a noble family of the Mâconnais ("from the region of Cluny" according to his biographer); but very little is known about the family, and there is a great deal of confusion in the secondary literature about Hugh's origins.

---

1. *Gesta*, p. 417. The literary topos of nobility of soul as equal to or greater than nobility of birth was a commonplace throughout the Middle Ages: see Ernst Robert Curtius, *European Literature and the Latin Middle Ages*, trans. William R. Trask (New York, 1953), pp. 179–80.

The names of his parents are unknown—the biographer left blanks in the text where the names should be. It is clear, however, that Hugh was not the count of Mâcon, as was claimed by the editors of *Gallia Christiana*;[2] the count at that time was named William. The only information on Hugh's youth comes from the *Vita prima* of St. Bernard. Hugh was a friend of the young Bernard, who persuaded Hugh to accompany him to Cîteaux. The *Vita prima* calls Hugh "an outstanding noble man from Mâcon," a phrase that seems to indicate that he was from one of the many families of castellans of the region (many of whom were named Hugh, after Abbot Hugh of Cluny).[3] There is no indication in the sources that Hugh was actually related to Bernard, although this has sometimes been claimed.[4] The *Vita prima* relates that Hugh, as a young knight, changed his mind about going to Cîteaux before the date set to enter the house, but that Bernard reconverted him in the middle of a rainstorm. There is a similar story of a rainstorm conversion of another Hugh, an elderly cleric named Hugh of Vitry, in the fragmentary *Vita tertia* of Bernard attributed to Geoffrey of Clairvaux; this Hugh of Vitry is not said to have become bishop of Auxerre, unlike Hugh of Mâcon in the *Vita prima*.[5] This account has led several modern authors to confuse Hugh of Mâcon with Hugh of Vitry, and has forced them to contrive explanations for how the same man could have been a young knight and an elderly cleric at the same time.[6]

Although Hugh of Mâcon may have suffered a brief lapse from his religious conversion, he seems to have shown a true enthusiasm and aptitude for monasticism once he reached Cîteaux in 1112. In 1114, he was made the first abbot of Pontigny, the second daughter house of Cîteaux. Pontigny prospered under him for twenty-two years, founding several

2. *Gallia Christiana* 12, col. 441.

3. *Vita prima Sancti Bernardi* 1.13-14, PL 185:235. Georges Duby, "Lignage, noblesse, et chevalerie au XIIe siècle dans la région mâconnaise," *Hommes et structures du moyen âge* (Paris, 1973), p. 419.

4. As by M. Terre, "L'élection à l'évêqué d'Auxerre du successeur du bienheureux Hughes de Mâcon," in *Mélanges Saint Bernard*, Association bourguignonne des sociétés savantes, XXIVe Congrès (Dijon, 1953), p. 116.

5. It is not clear whether the *Vita tertia* was written well after Bernard's death or whether, as some scholars have maintained, it is a series of notes written down during Bernard's lifetime on which the *Vita prima* is based. At any rate, the elderly cleric Hugh of the *Vita tertia* and the young knight Hugh of the *Vita prima* are clearly two different people, even if both are described as having a rainstorm conversion. See the *Vita tertia* text in Robert Lechat, "Les Fragmenta de vita et miraculis S. Bernardi," *Analecta Bollandiana* 50 (1932), 94-95.

6. Jean Mariller, "La vocation," in *Bernard de Clairvaux*, ed. Commission d'histoire de l'Ordre de Cîteaux (Paris, 1953), pp. 35-36. Gaetano Raciti, "Hughes de Mâcon (ou de Vitry)," *Dictionnaire de spiritualité*, 7, 1:886-89 [1969].

daughter houses and acquiring a great deal of property in the surrounding countryside.

This Cistercian abbot was immediately and unanimously chosen by the cathedral canons upon the death of Hugh of Montaigu, the bishop who had embraced the Cistercian way of life and was considered a saint, at least by his biographer. Hugh of Mâcon's election in 1136 is the first for which details survive concerning the manner of his election. Although the elections of his two predecessors had been contested, Hugh's biographer related that, within a week of Hugh of Montaigu's death, Hugh of Mâcon was elected unanimously, by clergy and people, with "the invocation of the Holy Spirit" (*facta invocatione Sancti Spiritus*). This inspired unanimity was, according to developing canon law, one of the three ways in which a bishop might be chosen; it was much simpler but also much rarer than the other two alternatives, a weighing of votes, called *scrutinium*, and a *compromissum* in which the election was entrusted to a few electors.[7] This election of 1136 was the last one for which the people of Auxerre were mentioned as playing any role in the choice of the bishop. All over France at this time, the clergy were gaining an electoral monopoly. Gratian, writing a few years after Hugh's election, concluded that laymen could only give assent to an election performed by the clergy and that indeed the absence of such assent had little effect on the new bishop's acquisition of jurisdictional and administrative powers.[8] Although there was no controversy over Hugh's election, there was some delay in his consecration. The archbishop of Sens, who normally would have consecrated him, had been temporarily suspended for continuing to hear witnesses in a case that had been appealed to Rome. Hugh was instead consecrated in 1137 in a ceremony at which the bishop of Chartres presided.[9]

Episcopal Rigor

"Evils were daily growing, and dangers to the church were multiplying," said the biographer. "Only a few prelates" could be found who would bring the "rigor of justice" against the wicked, in defense of their flock.[10] Hugh was clearly one of those few prelates, in his biographer's

---

7. *Gesta*, p. 417. Gabriel LeBras, *Institutions ecclésiastiques de la Chrétienté médiévale*, Histoire de l'église depuis les origines jusqu'à nos jours 12 (Paris, 1959–64), p. 372.

8. Robert L. Benson, *The Bishop-Elect* (Princeton, 1968), pp. 28–35. Emile Roland, *Les chanoines et les élections épiscopales de XIe au XIVe siècle* (Aurillac, 1909), p. 61.

9. *Gesta*, p. 417. Quantin 1.187, pp. 323–25.

10. *Gesta*, p. 417: "Cotidie enim crescit malicia et multiplicantur mala super ecclesiam,

estimation. He represented the chief enemies of the church of Auxerre as the counts of Nevers, William II and his son William III. Hugh of Mâcon, he indicated, had to act immediately upon taking office to recover property and rights from William II, which the count had obtained due to a "lack of justice" in Hugh of Montaigu.[11]

The biographer of Hugh of Montaigu, writing during Hugh of Mâcon's pontificate, did not mention that his subject had had any difficulty with the count. The surviving documents reveal that the chief differences between Hugh of Mâcon and William II were over the administration of justice in the city of Auxerre. Though control of justice meant final authority over the men of the city and a large amount of revenue, and thus was a highly sought-after right,[12] this dispute was not really over rights "belonging to the church by canonical right," as the biographer stated, for both bishop and count had a valid claim to administer justice in Auxerre. This quarrel was settled by the mediation of Hugh's old friend, Bernard of Clairvaux, who was someone both parties could trust, though he had no institutional ties to the diocese.

Bernard drew up a long charter in 1145 which stipulated that the bishop should have jurisdiction over all clerics in the city as well as his own *familia*, and the count jurisdiction over all laymen. Compromises were also reached on the city tolls and taxes, the establishment of guards for the vineyards, and the relative rights of bishop and count in the nearby woods of Bruyère.[13] In addition to these compromises Bernard spelled out an agreement between Hugh and William which established the count's dependence on the bishop, in a section which William's descendants would contest but would be forced to accept by Hugh's successors. William pledged that he would make no change or innovation (*mutatio vel innovatio*) in Auxerre without the bishop's permission and declared that he held the

---

quemadmodum pauci inveniuntur prelati in aecclesia Dei, qui animam pro grege sibi commisso contra malignantes obponant [cf. John 10.11] et rigorem justicie in laude bonorum et vindictam malorum exerceant."

11. Ibid., p. 418: "Comitem Willelmum . . . vocando in causam, ad hoc canonico judicio coegit, ut multa ecclesiae sue restitueret, que de jure canonicorum ecclesiae sue fuerant, multa etiam ad jus episcopale pertinentia quae idem comes, propter defectum justicie predecessoris sui, in suam redegerat potestatem."

12. Georges Duby, *Guerriers et paysans, VII–XIIe siècle: Premier essor de l'économie européenne* (Paris, 1973), p. 255.

13. This last included the maintenance of a hedged compound, wood-gathering, and hunting, rights of a sort commonly detailed in twelfth-century France when forests provided a valuable and vulnerable source of food, fuel, and pasturage. Michel Devize, "Forêts françaises et forêts allemandes: Etude historique comparée," *Revue historique* 235 (1966), 347–80, and 236 (1966), 47–68.

castles of Châteauneuf, St.-Sauveur, Cosne, and Mailly from the bishop in fief.[14] The bishop thus made himself, in the count's eyes and his own, the count's superior in temporal as well as spiritual power, even though he received nothing but homage for the castles, which were already in the count's possession.

The agreement in 1145 between Hugh and William was one of the first in which a bishop and count delineated precisely the separation of their rights and authority in the episcopal city, placing the count in a subordinate position on at least some issues. But in the following ten or fifteen years, bishops of other sees also gained some measure of supremacy over the local nobility: the bishop of Langres persuaded a number of castellans to do homage to him (including the counts of Nevers in their capacity as counts of Tonnerre); the archbishop of Lyon obtained an imperial bull distinguishing his land and rights from those of the count of Forez; the bishop of Agde and other bishops of the Narbonnaise obtained their cities' comital rights and had these rights confirmed by royal charters.[15] Fifty years after they had shaken themselves free from secular domination of ecclesiastical affairs, French bishops were gaining supremacy over the secular authorities in some aspects of secular justice and dominion.

William II was only count for one more year after Hugh had "compelled" him, in the biographer's words, to "restore many goods to the church." In 1146, encouraged by Bernard of Clairvaux, he retired to La Grande Chartreuse; he had been a benefactor of this house since its early years. Louis VII, who was leaving for the Holy Land, asked him to be regent of France with Suger, but William had already determined to go to Chartreuse. He died there in 1147 after one year as a *conversus* and nearly fifty years as count of Auxerre, Tonnerre, and Nevers. Since he had yielded readily to Hugh when Bernard prepared a compromise between them, and since he had a reputation in Paris as an honest and religious man, it is difficult to see in him a source of the "multiplying evils" attacking the church of Auxerre. His sons who succeeded him did not have a chance to attack Hugh at once—had they wished to—for they took the cross with Louis VII.

---

14. Quantin 1.247, pp. 393-97.
15. Michel Belotte, "Les possessions des évêques de Langres dans la région de Mussy-sur-Seine et de Châtillon-sur-Seine du milieu du XIIe au milieu du XIVe siècle," *Annales de Bourgogne* 37 (1965), 170-71. Marcel David, *Le patrimoine foncier de l'église de Lyon de 984 à 1267* (Lyon, 1942), pp. 15-16. André Castaldo, *L'église de Agde (Xe-XIIIe siècle)* (Paris, 1970), pp. 57-68. André Dupont, *Les cités de la Narbonnaise première, depuis les invasions germaniques jusqu'à l'apparition du consulat* (Nîmes, 1942), pp. 564-72. Agde's royal privilege was forged, but the other bishops of the Narbonnaise apparently obtained authentic privileges.

William III only returned from the Holy Land in 1149, and his brother Raynald never came back.[16] Even after William III returned, his deeds which the biographer describes scarcely seem to represent dangerous attacks on the church's position. The chief menace which the biographer indicated was William's denial that the bishop had any hunting rights in the woods of Montbar, near the city. Hugh replied by riding through the woods and then through the middle of Auxerre, under the count's eyes, with his hunters and dogs; this spectacle, according to the biographer, demonstrated Hugh's possession of hunting rights and allowed the bishop to retain them. Besides thus defending his rights, the biographer noted that Hugh also made some improvements to episcopal property. He bought one house next to the episcopal palace, from which the nightly raucousness of low persons (gartiones et ancille) had disturbed his sleep, and bought another house outside the palace gates. He also gave the chapter the outlying parish church of Lindry and 22 pounds to establish his anniversary.[17] But for the most part the biographer described Hugh's defense of his rights against laymen rather than gifts to ecclesiastics.

Hugh was clearly a bishop determined to have his own way. This characteristic may be seen again in his treatment of the churches of the diocese. "His endeavor was always to protect religious houses and to hold them in his hand and to reform to true religion the houses where the brothers pretended to religion only in the form of their habit."[18] Thus Hugh's biographer summarized Hugh's forceful but effective diocesan administration. As an example, he related that, around 1141, Hugh turned the canons of Notre-Dame-la-Dehors out of their church, as their way of life was not honorable (quorum conversatio minus erat honesta), and gave the church, "by his authority," to the Premonstratensians who had recently been established at St.-Marien. The biographer gave no further details on the Premonstratensians other than to say that Hugh had the count's help in establishing them in the city of Auxerre, but Robert of St.-Marien, a Premonstratensian chronicler writing at the end of the century, gave a full account. Calling

16. Bernard of Clairvaux, The Letters, trans. Bruno Scott James (London, 1953), pp. 309–10, nos. 230–31; these letters are not found in the Mabillon canon. Odo of Deuil, De profectione Ludovici VII in orientem 1, ed. Virginia Gingerick Berry (New York, 1948), p. 14. De glorioso rege Ludovico, Ludovici filio 10, ed. Auguste Molinier, Vie de Louis le Gros par Suger suivie de l'Histoire du roi Louis VII (Paris, 1887), p. 158. Hugh of Poitiers, Origo et historia brevis Nivernensium comitum, ed. R. B. C. Huygens, Monumenta Vizeliacensia, Corpus Christianorum Continuatio Mediaevelis 42 (Turnhout, 1976), pp. 238–39.

17. Gesta, pp. 418–19.

18. Ibid., p. 419: "Studium etiam huius erat loca religiosa semper tueri et manu tenere et solo habitu religionem pretendentes ad religionis veritatem . . . reformare."

the two benefactors, Bishop Hugh and Count William, "men of praise-worthy life and powerful in the world," he recorded that Premonstraten-sian canons had first come to Auxerre at the invitation of the bishop and the count in 1139, to settle in the newly restored church of St.-Marien, under Rainer, the provost of Prémontré. Hugh and William shortly agreed to give the canons the priory of Notre-Dame, to which most of the canons moved permanently, as St.-Marien was small and cramped. Hugh also gave the canons the long-abandoned church of St.-Martin, near St.-Marien, the revenues from another outlying parish church, a mill outside the city, and a prebend in the cathedral chapter.[19]

Although the biographer did not mention it specifically, Hugh's docu-ments indicate other actions of the bishop for the good of local houses. He gave the church of St.-Gervais, across the river from the cathedral and near St.-Marien and St.-Martin, to the monks of Molesme. At the same time, he established that the nuns of Crisenon, who were living in what had once been a priory of Molesme, should owe obedience to that monas-tery.[20] With the establishment of Premonstratensian canons in St.-Marien, St.-Martin, and Notre-Dame, and the submission of St.-Gervais to Molesme, Hugh completed the process begun by Humbaud of restoring the old aban-doned abbeys of the see and settling them with canons or monks following a strict rule. In his biographer's words, he had "reformed them to true religion."

The biographer summed up Hugh's effectiveness by stating that, "according to the assessment of the wise," Hugh's integrity and good advice made him "outstanding among all the bishops of Gaul."[21] Although the biographer gave no examples of Hugh's wider influence in the French church, it is clear from other sources that Hugh was indeed considered a good man to arbitrate quarrels between ecclesiastics, outside as well as in-side his own diocese. The quarrels which he helped mediate when called out of his diocese ranged from ones involving simple townsmen to ones in-volving the most powerful figures in the kingdom. In 1138 he settled a dispute between two townsmen of Chablis; in 1140 he and a number of other ecclesiastics were asked to arbitrate a quarrel between King Louis VII and his chancellor; in 1144 he and the bishops of Paris and Soissons mediated a quarrel between the houses of St.-Victor and St.-Martin of

19. Robert of St.-Marien, pp. 231–35. Quantin 1.238, pp. 382–83. Quantin 2.134, p. 145.
20. Quantin 2.49, pp. 54–55.
21. *Gesta*, p. 419: "... inter universos Gallicane ecclesie coepiscopos precipue honestatis et magni consilii pro certo sapientum judicio. . . ."

Paris; in 1148, at the Council of Reims that condemned Gilbert de la Porrée, Hugh was chosen, with Suger and the bishop of Morins, to prepare a statement of faith against which Gilbert's profession of faith would be compared.[22]

In his own diocese, Hugh's documents indicate that he often mediated quarrels between local houses or between those houses and laymen. He mediated a quarrel between the Cistercian houses of Pontigny and Reigny over pasture rights, settled a quarrel between Pontigny and St.-Germain over some woods that had been given to Pontigny (he decided in favor of St.-Germain rather than his old abbey), and stopped the incessant quarreling over parish rights between the churches of St.-Pierre and St.-Pèlerin of Auxerre by the drastic measure of uniting their parishes (the two churches are about 150 meters apart).[23] He reached settlements favorable to the monks of St.-Germain when they quarreled with three knights of Maligny in 1148 and with Geoffrey, lord of Donzy, in 1151, and he forced one Heldric of Vincelles to restore some tithes to St.-Marien in 1151, an agreement enforced by the count.[24] Hugh also frequently witnessed gifts from laymen to the local monasteries, especially Pontigny, and in at least some of these cases he suggested the gift himself; Count William made a gift of land to St.-Marien in 1144, saying it was "at the suggestion of Lord Hugh, bishop of Auxerre," and at Hugh's insistence, the sons of Landric de Préhy confirmed their father's gifts to Pontigny, after a long period of refusing to recognize them.[25] Pressure from Hugh, perhaps promising indulgence for whatever crime he had accused them of, may well have motivated other donors as well, though this motivation is hidden by the stylized words, "for the salvation of my soul and my ancestors'." The documents attesting to these actions, which are merely those surviving out of all those Hugh issued, support the biographer's generalized description of a bishop renowned for his judgment.

Yet the documents indicate that there was another aspect to Hugh's concern for ecclesiastical justice, one the biographer did not mention: he was determined to defend his own rights against other churchmen, even if

22. Quantin 1.191, pp. 329–30. Achille Luchaire, *Etudes sur les acts de Louis VII* (Paris, 1885), pp. 120–21, no. 67. Jules Tardif, ed., *Monuments historiques* (Paris, 1886), pp. 256–57, no. 471; and Arch. Nat. L 888A, nos. 14–15. Geoffrey of Clairvaux, *De condemnatione Gilberti Porret*, PL 185:591–92.

23. Quantin 1.264, 253, 222, pp. 416–17, 404, 365–66.

24. Ibid., 1.286, 328, pp. 440–41, 480–81. Arch. Yonne H 1290. Quantin 1.335, pp. 489–90. Although popes and councils had by now been repeating for three generations that laymen should not hold tithes, some laymen would continue to claim the right to do so through the thirteen century; Heldric was not alone.

25. Quantin 1.238, 241, pp. 382, 385–86.

it meant a prolonged quarrel. This attitude is seen most clearly in Hugh's dispute with Peter the Venerable, abbot of Cluny, over who should approve and appoint new abbots of the Cluniac house of St.-Germain.

Not long after his election, Hugh had Pope Innocent II confirm that any abbot of St.-Germain, once elected, blessed, and invested, would owe the bishop obedience and reverence.[26] But the question of who should actually bless and invest, the bishop of Auxerre or the abbot of Cluny, arose when Abbot Gervais died in 1148. There had not been an earlier opportunity for bishop and abbot to quarrel over the head of St.-Germain, since Gervais was only the second Cluniac abbot, and he had been invested by Bishop Hugh of Montaigu, his predecessor as abbot of the house. The quarrel of 1148 was appealed to the pope, and Eugenius III arranged a compromise: the approval of the abbot of Cluny would be necessary before a newly elected abbot of St.-Germain could be blessed by the bishop, but only the bishop would invest the new abbot with his staff.[27]

Hugh accepted this compromise, but his determination to retain control over diocesan churches led to another quarrel with Peter the Venerable the following year, this time over the Cluniac house of La Charité. Hugh had already asserted his rights over this house in 1138, preventing the Cluniac bishop of Troyes, Hato, from performing ordinations there.[28] In 1149, the prior of La Charité complained that Hugh was appropriating his tithes, churches, and cattle; Hugh replied that the prior was diverting episcopal property to illicit purposes and asked Peter the Venerable to remove him. The prior seems to have remained in office for a few more years, and the outcome of the quarrel is not clear.[29]

It is clear that Hugh's pursuit of ecclesiastical justice, while making him a zealous reformer of local churches and a valued mediator outside the diocese, also brought him into quarrels with other ecclesiastics which his biographer preferred to let pass unnoted. But Hugh's charters taken together (the ones in which he helped the local churches outnumber by far his quarrels) tend to confirm his biographer's approving assessment of him as a bishop "efficacious and prompt" in administrative affairs.[30]

---

26. Ibid., 1.218, pp. 361–62.
27. Ibid., 1.288, pp. 442–43. *Gallia Christiana* 12:122–23, no. 32.
28. Peter the Venerable, Letters 69, 71, ed. Giles Constable (Cambridge, Mass., 1967), 1:200, 204–05.
29. Suger, Letter 71, RHGF 15:510. John F. Benton, "An Abusive Letter of Nicolas of Clairvaux for a Bishop of Auxerre, Possibly Blessed Hugh of Mâcon," *Mediaeval Studies* 33 (1971), 365–70. Constable, *The Letters of Peter the Venerable*, 2: 296–98.
30. *Gesta*, p. 417.

Hugh of Mâcon's administrative acts—his defense of episcopal rights against the count and his frequent arbitration in cases involving local houses and also other French dioceses—were much more numerous than those of his predecessor. Hugh of Montaigu had not himself quarreled with any laymen, and, as far as the records show, no churches of Auxerre quarreled with other churches during his pontificate, and only one church quarreled with a layman. Hugh of Mâcon left nearly twice as many documents as his predecessor from a pontificate two years shorter, and these documents show a greater legalism and concern for specific rights. An example of the differences can be seen by comparing two charters in which knights gave property, located at Ste.-Porcaire, to Pontigny.[31] In the first one, issued by Hugh of Montaigu early in his pontificate, the land to be given is described in very simple terms; the only verb of donation is a single *dedisse*; there are eight witnesses; the charter was composed and written by the bishop himself (*per manum meam*); and the year is not given. In the second, issued by Hugh of Mâcon in 1146, although fewer pieces of land are being given, they are described in detail as including "wooded and open land, meadows, and waters"; the knights not only "give" the land, but "grant" that the monks shall have it "in perpetuity, freely, and without argument," and further "promise by their faith" that they themselves shall not settle their men on this land nor try to cultivate it; there are twelve witnesses; the bishop's clerk, rather than the bishop himself, drew up the charter, which is dated by the Year of the Incarnation and is in all about twice as long as the first.

These differences, though they may in part be differences in the personal styles of the two bishops, reflect the growing legalism of the age. Hugh of Mâcon was bishop at a time when most French bishops were acquiring a large staff of clerics and lawyers, becoming heads of increasingly complex jurisdictional and administrative machinery. Studies of episcopal charters from England have demonstrated that during the course of the twelfth century, episcopal, papal, and royal charters all became more stylized and uniform. During Hugh's pontificate, Gratian's *Decretum* and Peter Lombard's *Sentences* were compiled to give a more orderly synthesis of legal questions and theological opinions.[32]

Part of the increase in complexity of episcopal administration in the first half of the twelfth century was a reaction to the growing influence of

31. Quantin 1.130, 259, pp. 244–45, 410.
32. R. W. Southern, *Western Society and the Church in the Middle Ages* (Harmondsworth, Eng., 1970), p. 189. C. R. Cheney, *English Bishops' Chanceries, 1100–1250* (Manchester, 1950), pp. 3–4. David Knowles, *The Evolution of Medieval Thought* (New York, 1962), pp. 176–83.

papal government. Though Hugh's biographer never mentioned the pope, the bishop's charters reveal that the affairs of the diocese of Auxerre were coming increasingly under papal scrutiny. The papal curia was the court of first appeal in Hugh's 1148 quarrel over St.-Germain. The pope was called in to help settle a quarrel between St.-Germain and the abbey of Vézelay, when St.-Germain held prisoner some men dependent on Vézelay. When the dean of the cathedral of Auxerre was excommunicated around 1140 (for a reason that is not clear), Hugh had Bernard write directly to the pope to ask for his absolution. The pope twice confirmed the rights and possessions of Pontigny and also confirmed the rights of Reigny and St.-Germain, in all cases without specific request of the bishop, though such an episcopal request had been normal earlier. Innocent II even united the collegiate chapter of St.-Florentin to the house of St.-Germain without specific mention of the bishop.[33]

Increased involvement by the pope in local affairs was typical of many sees in the years after 1130. Papal administrative machinery grew even faster than did the bishops'. Innocent II (1130–1143) issued an average of twice as many surviving charters per year as his immediate predecessors, and the yearly average doubled again by 1160. Around the time of Hugh of Mâcon's death, Bernard wrote to Eugenius III that he was spending all his time in listening to a steady stream of litigants coming to the Roman curia, with no good results. After about 1140, the pope was increasingly called on to adjudicate cases rather than simply to confirm privileges, as had been the case earlier.[34] Episcopal independence in local administration was also decreased by ecumenical councils. The Second Lateran Council, which Innocent II held in 1139, produced a great deal of elaborate legislation on such issues as the study of law and medicine by monks and canons regular, tournaments, nuns living without a rule, the inheritance of ecclesiastical goods, and the use of crossbows (it is impossible to say whether Hugh attended this council since no list of participants survives). The First Lateran Council, held sixteen years earlier, had issued little more than half as many canons (17 vs. 30), most of them on the topic of reforming clerical abuses, rather than on the broader issues of Christian life.[35] Regional councils, too, helped determine local diocesan affairs.

33. Quantin 1.236, p. 380. Bernard of Clairvaux, Letter 215, PL 182:379. Quantin 1.189, 217, 282, 327, 190, pp. 326–27, 359–61, 435–36, 478–80, 327–28.

34. Southern, *Western Society and the Church*, pp. 109, 115. Bernard of Clairvaux, *De Consideratione* 1.1–2, *Opera*, ed. Jean Leclercq and Henri Rochais, 3 (Rome, 1963), 394–97.

35. Hefele–Leclercq, *Histoire des conciles*, 5, 1:631–39, 725–33. Raymonde Foreville, *Latran I, II, III et Latran IV* (Paris, 1965), pp. 175–78, 187–94.

Hugh was present in 1141 at the Council of Sens, which condemned Peter Abelard, as well as at the Council of Reims in 1148.[36]

The biographer did not mention any influence the pope or councils might have had on Hugh's administration; this information comes from other sources. Nor did he mention any role the archbishop, the king, or the count may have had in the ecclesiastical affairs of Auxerre, but here the documents give a similar picture. The archbishop and the king occasionally passed through the diocese—Louis VII met Thibaut of Champagne at Auxerre to make peace with that count in 1138—but their role in local affairs remained small.[37] The count's role was primarily to support the bishop's decisions as when he helped found and endow St.-Marien or enforced an agreement between St.-Marien and some knights (see above). The only real challenge to the authority of Hugh and other French bishops of his time came from the pope. But the biographer, who described Hugh as holding the local churches firmly in his hand, pictured a bishop without rival in his ordering of diocesan affairs.

In only one instance did the biographer express sharp disapproval of one of Hugh's acts: the nepotism scandal over Hugh's restoration of the office of provost. Hugh of Montaigu had suppressed the office of provost and given the revenues of the office to the cathedral canons, having the pope confirm that this agreement would be observed in perpetuity (see above, Chapter II). Hugh of Mâcon, however, restored the office and gave it to his nephew Stephen, taking back the revenues of the provost's prebend from the chapter. He asked Bernard to write the pope on his nephew's behalf, since the gift of the provostry to the chapter had been papally confirmed and needed papal approval to be overturned; later, when Stephen tried to make himself bishop after his uncle's death, Bernard said that he had never intended that Hugh overturn the gift of the provostry to the chapter but had only wanted to help Stephen advance.[38]

The biographer, a member of the chapter who had benefited from the revenues of the provost's prebend, stated that Hugh of Montaigu's suppression of the office had been motivated by "the kindest affection and love," "for the common good of the brothers," and that it had been confirmed as solidly as possible by the authority of the pope and of St. Stephen, the protomartyr. He indicated that in thus making his nephew provost, Hugh of Mâcon seriously damaged his reputation for good judgment: "He would have been considered outstanding among the bishops of Gaul, since

36. Hefele–Leclercq, *Histoire des conciles*, 5, 1:754.
37. *De glorioso rege Ludovico, Ludovici filio* 5, ed. Molinier, p. 151.
38. Letter 274, PL 182:480.

he was very solicitous of the goods of the church, except that he gave a certain nephew of his the provostry. . . ."[39] The biographer of Hugh of Montaigu, writing during the episcopate of Hugh of Mâcon, viewed the affair in very much the same light. He mentioned that Hugh of Mâcon did not honor his predecessor's gift to the church immediately after extolling Hugh of Montaigu for "never giving his nephew a prebend." He did not specifically include Hugh of Mâcon among the multitudes of unnamed prelates who, in contrast to Hugh of Montaigu, "gave prebends to unworthy relatives," but his point was clear.[40] Hugh of Mâcon, reacting to the canons' objections, described his chapter in very abusive terms, in the same letter in which he asked Peter the Venerable to remove the prior of La Charité. He said that the *antiquissimus serpens* had caused members of the chapter to impugn his innocence and that they certainly could not judge him since they themselves were guilty of sexual crimes (there is no other evidence for such a charge).[41]

Hugh's insistence on bestowing the revived office of provost on his nephew, over the canons' objections, seems to have grown out of the same tendency to impose his own will that had led him to turn the "dishonorable" canons of Notre-Dame-la-Dehors out of their house and to ride through the middle of Auxerre with his hunters and hounds to force the count to recognize his hunting rights. In this case, however, the biographer could not approve the results.

Rigor vs. Humility

There are also indications that the biographer did not always agree with Hugh's methods in some of his other activities, even though he could applaud the result. Though he described approvingly Hugh's firm stand against the local nobility and his reform of diocesan churches, he seems to have felt uneasy about the lack of humility which these actions displayed. He went to some lengths to justify this lack. "Too much humility," he said,

39. *Gesta*, p. 419: ". . . cuidam tamen nepoto suo preposituram . . . benignissimo caritatis affectu, venerabilis bone memorie Hugo predecessor suus ad bonum commune fratrum super mensam Sancti Stephani per manum eiusdem prothomartyris dederat."
40. Ibid., pp. 415–16: "et cum inter omnes prelatos, aecclesiae cuiuscumque fuerint ordinis, vix unus possit inveniri, qui parentes suos, etiam si non sint digni, non sublimet honoribus et beneficiis ecclesiarum, iste singularis inter infinitos cuidam suo nepoti nunquam in vita sua prebendam voluit dare."
41. Benton, "Abusive Letter," supposes that Hugh may have used several churches he had acquired during his pontificate to reestablish the revenues for the office of provost; it seems more likely that Hugh simply reappropriated the revenues that Hugh of Montaigu had given the chapter as a whole.

was inappropriate for a bishop, for it could only "diminish evil men's respect for the sword of St. Peter." He seemed aware that Hugh's behavior, especially when pressing his rights against the local nobility, might be construed as lacking in the humility proper for a Cistercian bishop; when describing how Hugh was accustomed to avert his eyes from the castellans who came on their knees before him to beg absolution, he hastened to add that this reaction was not due to any "pride or disdain," but was rather Hugh's method for assuring proper respect for the church.[42] Defense of the church's rights against marauders certainly needed no vindication; Gregory the Great had put it among the necessary attributes of a bishop, along with humility.[43] The biographer only felt a need to justify Hugh's actions because, when Hugh "used the rigor of his justice to trample" those who had laid hands on church property, he "laid aside his humility and patience," which he did not always find sufficient for a victory.[44]

The biographer's insistence that there were compelling reasons why Hugh was not more humble seems to indicate that he was aware of the large body of contemporary opinion that a religious man should be humble, especially a member of Hugh's own Cistercian order. Bernard of Clairvaux constantly insisted that humility and renunciation of one's will were the only way to the love of God. The Cistercian chapter general of 1134 established that Cistercian monks who became bishops must keep to the humble standards of their order in food and clothing, though they were allowed a second cope. The second-generation Cistercian Isaac of Stella (c. 1115–1169) insisted in his writings that the virtuous life had to begin with humility.[45] Contemporary authors who were not Cistercians also emphasized humility as a requirement for holiness. Peter Lombard in his *Sentences* made pride the root of all other deadly sins. The biographer

42. *Gesta*, pp. 418-19: "Cumque multociens castellani et potentiores ad presentiam suam venientes, pro indulgentia alicujus commissi requirenda et genuflexu preces funderent, non statim illis responsum dabat, immo etiam aliquando oculos suos ab eis videbatur avertere, non propter superbiam, vel indignationem, sed ne nimia humilitas que talibus placere non potest, in gladio Petri timoris minueret reverentiam."

43. *Regula Pastoralis* 1.5, PL 77:18.

44. *Gesta*, p. 417: ". . . et quos non poterat per patientiam et humilitatem superare, conculcabat rigore justicie, qui, judicio sapientis, multum necessarius semper est in aecclesia Dei."

45. Etienne Gilson, *The Mystical Theology of Saint Bernard*, trans. A. H. C. Downes (New York, 1940), p. 30. François Vandenbrouke, *La morale monastique du XIe au XVIe siècle* (Louvain, 1966), p. 154. Paul Remy Oliger, *Les évêques réguliers* (Paris, 1958), pp. 114-16. See especially Bernard's *Liber de gradibus humilitatis et superbiae, Opera*, 3:13-59. For Isaac of Stella, see Bernard McGinn, *The Golden Chain* (Washington, D.C., 1972).

of Hugh of Montaigu, writing during Hugh of Mâcon's pontificate, had made humility the chief attribute of a man undoubtedly among the saints. William Godellus, writing at Sens around 1170, found that the best way to praise Hugh of Mâcon, whom he had not known personally but knew to be a Cistercian, was to call him a man "based in the humility of holy religion."[46]

Thus, when Hugh's biography was composed shortly after his death in 1151 (it is copied in the same hand as his successor's early charters), the prevailing contemporary opinion was that a monk, even a monk-bishop like Hugh, should display humility. Yet in the biographer's eyes, Hugh did not demonstrate this virtue. Unlike his predecessor, he had had little opportunity to learn humility and obedience; he spent his youth not as an oblate but in training for knighthood and became abbot of Pontigny after living under an abbot for only two years at Cîteaux. The only virtue on which the biographer dwelt was Hugh's hospitality—the same virtue Humbaud's biographer had emphasized. He said that hospitality had been recommended "by both Jesus and St. Paul," and Hugh accordingly promised to be hospitable as part of his coronation oath, even setting a *conversus* from Pontigny in the episcopal palace to welcome visitors when he himself was away.[47] Though he said vaguely that Hugh had many "other virtues" as well, the biographer, unlike the biographer of Hugh of Montaigu, never called his subject *sanctus*.[48]

The biographer interspersed throughout his discussion of Hugh's administrative achievements examples of precedents for Hugh's unbending opposition to laymen who threatened the secular property of the church. He cited Augustine's remark that a bishop should correct sinners with rigor and Ambrose's example in forbidding Theodosius entry into the church because of his sins. He quoted Jerome's statement that one does actual harm to the church in failing to resist those who would destroy it and mentioned Phineas's firm stand for justice, which placated the Lord (Psalm 106.30, cf. Num. 25.7-8).[49] In using the Fathers of the church as

---

46. Morton W. Bloomfield, *The Seven Deadly Sins* (Lansing, 1967), pp. 72–85. William Godellus, *Chronicon*, RHGF 13:676.

47. *Gesta*, p. 419. Part of the twelfth-century ordination ritual for a bishop was the question, "Will you welcome pilgrims and the poor?" Michel Andrieu, ed., *Le Pontifical romain au moyen âge*, 1, *Le Pontifical romain du XIIe siècle* (Vatican City, 1958), p. 143.

48. Chevalier, *Bio-Bibliographie*, 1:2208, refers to Hugh as "Beatus," but there is no indication of a contemporary cult, and no other modern reference work (even AASS) considers him "Blessed." Chevalier probably confused Hugh of Mâcon with his predecessor, Hugh of Montaigu.

49. *Gesta*, pp. 417–18. Jerome, Letter 53, PL 22:542.

precedents for Hugh, the biographer avoided pointing out the fact that they were defending the faith and purity of the church, not its temporal possessions. He applauded Hugh's rigor, but he felt compelled to justify it at length when it kept the bishop from showing humility.

It must be pointed out that Hugh was not alone among contemporary bishops in his rigorous pursuit of the interests of his church, even when this pursuit required that humility be sacrificed. Bishop Otto of Bamberg (1103–1139), holy enough to be considered a saint after his death, was described by his biographer Ebbo as having converted the Pomeranians successfully only because he rejected poverty and humility (specifically including Jesus' admonitions in Luke 10.4) and went instead with a great display of wealth and power. The Cistercian bishop John of Valence, like Hugh, was described by his biographer as defending episcopal property and recovering through the exercise of justice that which had been lost; unlike Hugh, however, John was said to possess the two separate qualities of personal holiness and effectiveness in episcopal administration, a combination his biographer called very rare.[50]

The combination was rare because it was very difficult in practice for any man to combine success in complex administrative duties and personal holiness, as defined to include withdrawal and humility. Hugh's friend Bernard certainly faced this problem in his own life, in that he tried to combine his search for holiness in the quiet of Clairvaux with the administrative duties of the Cistercian order (and indeed the cares of much of Christian society) that he felt obligated to assume. That he considered fulfilling one's administrative duties as essential may be seen in his writings as well as his life. In two sermons and a *vita* on the Irish saint Malachi, Bernard described this saintly bishop as resisting tyrants, ending the dangers to the church, and bringing peace.[51] Like Hugh's biographer, Bernard sometimes used the biblical figure of Phineas as an example of an ecclesiastical administrator who vigorously defended his church from heresy and evil inclinations.[52] Bernard seems to have considered Hugh to be an excellent bishop; he is never known to have reprimanded him for lack of humility, and after Hugh's death, unlike the biographer, Bernard described him to the pope as a *sanctus vir* and a *sanctus episcopus*.[53] Though these phrases may only indicate respect for his late friend, their use indicates

50. Ebbo, *Vita Ottonis episcopi Babenbergensis* 2.1–2, MGH SS 12:841–43. Giraud, *Vita S. Johannis Valentiensis episcopi*, RHGF 14:319–20.

51. PL 183:485. *Opera*, ed. Leclercq and Rochais, 6, 1:51–53. *De vita et rebus gestis S. Malachiae*, *Opera* 3:361–64.

52. Letters 158, 213, 276, PL 182:316, 378, 482.

53. Letter 276, PL 182:481. *De consideratione* 3.2.11, *Opera* 3:438.

that Bernard did not feel that Hugh's pursuit of justice, in such secular areas as the agreement with the count that Bernard himself mediated,[54] decreased his personal sanctity. The biographer, who witnessed some of Hugh's activities at closer hand, seems to have felt more sharply the effect that a strong defense of episcopal rights had on Hugh's sanctity, but like Bernard he still considered administrative ability essential in a bishop.

Conclusions

Hugh's biography and existing charters give a picture of a vigorous and very thorough bishop, with a reputation for good judgment, who rigorously defended the rights of local churches and his own. Unlike his predecessor, who had been content to administer the affairs of the diocese between retreats to the cloister and had never quarreled with the local nobility, Hugh spent all his time as bishop involved in the increasingly complex administrative tasks that faced many French bishops in the years before 1150 and in pressing his rights against the local nobility. He is not known to have returned to Pontigny except for brief (and official) visits, until in 1151 he returned there to die. His biographer's description of the challenges he faced, the daily multiplication of dangers to church property, laymen with small respect for the sword of Peter, and unceasing enmity from Count William II is in sharp contrast with the placid scene described by the biographer of Hugh of Montaigu. In part the two bishops had different estimations of their duties and thus of the challenges that faced them; in part the two biographers, each of whom clearly distinguished his own bishop's activities from the failings of the other Bishop Hugh, emphasized those aspects of their subjects' pontificates which made their behavior seem most laudable. Thus Hugh of Mâcon may well have faced more attacks from laymen than his predecessor, but the biographer's account of a desperate time when "too much" humility had to be avoided still seems over-dramatized.

Hugh of Mâcon was succeeded by Alain, another Cistercian abbot, but one of undoubted humility. The fact that Hugh's biographer wrote during Alain's rule may be partially responsible for his long explanations of why Hugh was not more humble. But Alain's lack of the administrative ability was to make him unfit for the episcopacy, in the eyes of some contemporaries and certainly his own.

---

54. Although he himself spoke strongly against bishops' attempts to dominate their cities. *Tractatus de moribus et officio episcoporum, Opera*, ed. Leclercq and Rochais, 7:106.

IV

ALAIN,
THE RELUCTANT BISHOP

Alain (1152–1167), the third consecutive abbot to become bishop of Auxerre, was characterized by a love of the withdrawn monastic life. Yet unlike
Hugh of Montaigu, he did not find it possible simultaneously to withdraw
to the cloister and to administer the diocese. He was a stranger to Auxerre,
who certainly had had no ambition to become bishop there, and he was
the only twelfth-century bishop of Auxerre to resign. His most noteworthy
achievement was the *Vita secunda* of St. Bernard, written in the years
following his resignation. His anonymous biography is by far the shortest
produced in twelfth-century Auxerre, only some 250 words long; most of
it is a list of gifts he made to the local churches.

Little is known of Alain's origins, other than that he came from Flanders; it is not even known whether his family was noble. He had a brother
for whom he established an anniversary at a collegiate church outside Auxerre, but even this brother's name is unknown.[1] Some of our ignorance
about the details of Alain's early life is due to the confessed ignorance of
his biographer, who may not even have known Alain personally; his biography is written in the same hand as that of Alain's successor, who died in
1181, and it was probably composed hastily at the same time as that
biography.

Alain had become a monk under Bernard at Clairvaux as a young man,
and in 1140 he became the first abbot of the new Cistercian house of Larrivour, near Troyes. He passed an obscure decade there until Hugh of Mâcon
died in 1151. Hugh's death sparked a very complicated controversy over
the disposition of his goods and the selection of his successor. Alain's
biographer did not mention the controversy, but the details can be reconstructed from Bernard of Clairvaux's letters on the subject.[2] Hugh's nephew
Stephen, whom he had made provost, claimed that he should inherit most

---

1. "Obituaires de l'église collégiale de Ste.-Eugénie de Varzy," ed. August Longnon,
   Alexandre Vidier, and Léon Mirot, *Obituaires de la province de Sens*, 3, *Diocèses
   d'Orléans, d'Auxerre, et de Nevers* (Paris, 1909), p. 416.
2. In the following paragraphs, I have relied principally on Letters 274–76, 280, and
   282 of Bernard, PL 182:480–82, 485–89, and on the *De Consideratione* 3.2.11,
   Opera, ed. Jean Leclercq and Henri Rochais, 3 (Rome, 1963), 438–39. This election

of what the late bishop had acquired in episcopal goods, including seven churches and various tithes as well as meadows, woods, coins, and houses. Hugh actually seems to have made Stephen his heir when he fell sick a year before his death, but on recovering he had repudiated this will, and he died intestate. The rest of the chapter denied Stephen's claims to his uncle's goods, and he prepared to go to Rome to plead his case, demanding that no new bishop be elected until the question of his uncle's inheritance was settled.

The rest of the chapter proceeded to hold an election anyway, but they became irreconcilably split over two cathedral canons. Stephen and a few of his friends in the chapter then held an election of their own, in which Stephen himself was elected. Though only two canons would admit to electing Stephen when Bernard sent a monk to investigate the situation shortly thereafter, Stephen quickly gained the support of Count William III of Nevers and took custody of the episcopal seal. When two leaders of the local clergy of Auxerre, the dean of St.-Pierre and the prior of St.-Eusèbe, tried to go to Rome to inform the pope of the controversy, they were forcibly detained by the count, but they did manage to get word to Bernard.

Eugenius III, informed by Bernard of the situation, appointed three arbiters, including the abbot of Clairvaux, to choose the new bishop of Auxerre. Rejecting all three candidates elected by various factions of the chapter, Bernard and one of the other two arbiters selected Alain, abbot of Larrivour, and Eugenius supported their choice. Though Alain was thus the only twelfth-century bishop of Auxerre not elected by the local clergy, Bernard wrote Eugenius that he was acclaimed by the "wiser" part of the clergy and the people.

The count was soon reconciled to the new bishop, apparently by Bernard. Bernard also persuaded Louis VII to accept the election; Louis had maintained that although he gave his assent to holding an election when Hugh died, his permission should have been asked again before the final selection was made because of the dissent in the original election. This is the first time that the royal permission to elect (*licentia eligendi*) is mentioned in connection with Auxerre; Louis VII had had Innocent II confirm in 1139 that his permission must be asked before any episcopal election

---

has been described by almost everyone who discusses twelfth-century episcopal elections in France; each reconstruction of the events that has been given is somewhat different, due to the rather obscure nature of the sources. What follows is my own account.

was held in his kingdom.[3] This was the French parallel to the situation in the Empire, where, after the Concordat of Worms in 1122, elections were to be held in the emperor's presence.

Bernard told the king that he had chosen Alain because he was good (*bonus*), a term on which he did not elaborate.[4] Though Bernard does not seem to have questioned whether the qualities that made a good Cistercian abbot would also make a good bishop, Alain soon did, with the conclusion that the religious life he had chosen for himself when he entered Clairvaux, a life of prayer and study, was incompatible with the responsibilities he assumed when he became bishop of Auxerre. He repeatedly asked the pope for permission to resign his office, though his requests were repeatedly denied.

He was not the first to find the office of bishop incompatible with the life of a monk. Nearly a century earlier, Peter Damian had said that a monk who becomes a bishop is occupied with the affairs of the world and thus ceases to be a monk. The biographer of St. Anselm, writing in the first years of the twelfth century, indicated that the monastic virtues Anselm cultivated, humility, patience, and abstinence, were appropriate for a monk but not an archbishop. More recently, Abelard, drawing on St. Jerome, had said that a monk's elevation to the episcopate was a step downward in merit and saintliness.[5]

Alain was the first of the bishops of Auxerre from the regular clergy to be so struck by the incompatibility of the monastic life and episcopal duties that he found it necessary to resign for the sake of his spiritual well-being. His biographer, whether or not he knew Alain personally, made a statement consistent with Alain's actions when he said that he had already renounced the world and the *vita activa* once when he became a monk and that as bishop he constantly yearned to remove himself from the world and to resume the *vita contemplativa*. In 1167, when the pope would still not grant his request, Alain, pleading debility of mind and body, persuaded the archbishop to allow him to resign. The archbishop granted Alain's request without asking papal permission; by the time Alexander II learned of the abdication, Alain was back at Clairvaux, and the Auxerre cathedral chapter had elected the archbishop's brother as their new bishop.[6] In spite

3. Bernard Jacqueline, *Papauté et épiscopat selon Saint Bernard de Clairvaux* (Paris, 1963), p. 78.
4. Letter 282, PL 182:488-89.
5. Eadmer, *Vita Sancti Anselmi archiepiscopi Cantuariensis* 2.12, ed. R. W. Southern (London, 1962), p. 79. For Abelard, see his Sermon 33, PL 178:582-607, especially col. 599: "vita monastica praeminat episcopali administrationi."
6. *Gesta,* p. 420. Alexander III, Letter 468, PL 200:466.

of Alain's professed debility, he lived at least another fifteen years and immediately began writing the *Vita secunda* of Bernard.

Resignations were very rare in twelfth-century France; the majority of bishops died in their original sees, and translation rather than abdication accounted for most of those who did not. A bishop was considered married to his church, from which he could not be separated by divorce, only by death.[7] Bernard of Clairvaux, dead fifteen years by the time Alain resigned, had said in a letter to the bishop of York in 1138 that a bishop should not leave his church any more than a man should leave his wife. A desire for peace and quiet, he said, was not a sufficient excuse; the only excuse was the direct word of the pope or else a bishop's realization that he had committed a mortal sin. However, at least two other Cistercian bishops besides Alain resigned their sees, in the years after Bernard's death, when unable to resolve the conflict between their ideal of the holy life and the responsibilities of the episcopate. Bishop Peter of Tarentaise (1142–1174) left his see for a Cistercian house in 1155, after what his biographer described as a long interior monologue over the danger of becoming too accustomed to the world's honors and praises; but, unlike Alain, Peter returned to Tarentaise within the year, where his biographer described him constructing new buildings and reforming the clergy. Geoffrey, bishop of Langres (1139–1163), originally a monk of Clairvaux, resigned his see to return to that house. Another bishop, Bartholomew of Laon (1113–1150), though not originally a Cistercian, left his see permanently in 1150 for the Cistercian monastery of Foigny, out of "contempt for the world," according to the Premonstratensian chronicler who recorded his retreat.[8]

Withdrawal from the Cares of Office

There are few clues in Alain's brief biography to its author's views of how a man might seek salvation, but Alain revealed some of his own attitudes in his writings as well as in his resignation of the episcopate. He believed that the most holy life was the most withdrawn, the most separate from administrative cares. This view emerges from the revision of the *Vita*

7. Jean Gaudemet, "Recherches sur l'épiscopat médiéval en France," in *Proceedings of the Second International Congress of Medieval Canon Law*, ed. Stephan Kuttner and J. Joseph Ryan (Vatican City, 1965), p. 149. Gabriel LeBras, *Institutions ecclésiastiques de la Chrétienté médiévale*, Histoire de l'église depuis les origines jusqu'à nos jours 12 (Paris, 1959–64), p. 219. Jean-François Lemarignier, Jean Gaudemet, and Guillaume Mollat, *Institutions ecclésiastiques*, Histoire des institutions françaises au moyen âge 3 (Paris, 1962), p. 182.

8. Bernard of Clairvaux, Letter 20, PL 182:524. Geoffrey of Haute-Combe, *Vita Sancti Petri archiepiscopi Tarentasiensis*, AASS May 2:320–42. *Annales S. Benigni* 1166, MGH SS 5:45. *Sigiberti continuatio Praemonstratensis*, MGH SS 6:455.

of Bernard on which he worked after his resignation, a revision which emphasizes the saint's withdrawal from the world to a life of quiet contemplation. Though scarcely a word of the *Vita secunda* is Alain's own, he edited, condensed, and rearranged the *Vita prima*, which was begun during Bernard's life and continued by a series of different authors. His stated intention was to eliminate what was untrue and what was redundant; the initial impetus for the revision may have been the need perceived by the members of the Cistercian Order for a suitable *vita* to present to the Roman curia in preparation for Bernard's canonization (which took place in 1174). Yet the way that Alain transposed passages or eliminated sections suggests that he was doing more than just making a more accurate and readable *Vita*; he was giving his own picture of what a saintly life should be.[9]

As well as eliminating the personal references of the various authors of the *Vita prima* and many of the lists of miracles where Bernard healed a whole series of persons crippled or possessed by demons, Alain left out most of the sections on Bernard's wanderings through western Europe to end schisms and reconvert heretics. Although he gave an abbreviated account of Bernard's role in healing the schism of 1130, Alain did not describe Bernard, as had several of the authors of the *Vita prima*, as readily traveling to far-flung regions to care for and reform the church. He transposed some passages from sections which he otherwise eliminated and gave them special emphasis, passages on Bernard's love for a quiet life among the brothers, his flight from admiration and honor, and his desire to separate himself from business affairs (*negotiis*).[10] The first author of the *Vita prima*, William of St.-Thierry, who himself resigned as abbot of St.-Thierry to become a simple Cistercian monk and a scholar, had already described the monastic life of prayer and austerity as the way to rededicate the soul to God;[11] Alain went even further in emphasizing withdrawal and contemplation almost to the exclusion of Bernard's administrative activities for the church in the world.

At a time when the volume and complexity of episcopal business were increasing, it became much more difficult for a bishop to attend to the

9. *Vita prima*, PL 185:225-468. *Vita secunda*, ibid., 469-524. Jean Leclercq has pointed out that most twelfth-century saints' lives reveal more of the ideas of sanctity held by the author and his contemporaries than of the saint. *The Love of Learning and the Desire for God*, trans. Catharine Misrahi (New York, 1961), pp. 199-206.

10. See especially chapters 10, 14, and 26 of Alain's *Vita secunda*, and compare his work with the *Vita prima*, PL 185:487-88, 494, 250, 259.

11. Patrick Ryan, "The Witness of William of St.-Thierry to the Spirit and Aims of the Early Cistercians," in *The Cistercian Spirit: A Symposium in Memory of Thomas Merton*, ed. M. Basil Pennington (Spencer, Mass., 1970), pp. 228-30.

duties of his office if his view of the holy life required frequent retreats to the cloister. There are indications that by the mid-twelfth century cathedral chapters saw an incompatibility between the monastic life and episcopal duties, for they less and less frequently elected monks as bishops. In France, at the beginning of Louis VII's reign in 1137, 41% of the bishops whose ecclesiastical origins are known were from the regular clergy; at the end of his reign, in 1180, the figure had dropped to 18%. In England, the percentage of bishops from the regular clergy declined steadily from 33% to 0% between the late eleventh century and the end of the twelfth.[12] At Auxerre, Alain, who had succeeded two other abbots as bishop, was the last bishop chosen from the regular clergy until the end of the thirteenth century.

While the cathedral canons of the second half of the twelfth century were choosing a reduced number of monks to be their bishops, they were also choosing a reduced number of men holy enough to be considered saints after their deaths. The Roman curia canonized ten bishops from all of western Europe who died in the eleventh century, ten who died in the first half of the twelfth century, five in the second half of the twelfth century, and only nine for the whole thirteenth century, although the total number of saints canonized at Rome was rising. For those saints of western Christendom who were afforded a local cult although not formally canonized at Rome, the proportion of bishops among all saints dropped from 25% to 12% between the twelfth and thirteenth centuries.[13] In the dioceses of northern France (here defined as those lying within the medieval archdioceses of Besançon, Bordeaux, Lyon, Reims, Rouen, Sens, Tarentaise, and Vienne), I have found that the first half of the twelfth century produced nine bishop-saints afforded at least a local cult: Hugh of Grenoble (1080-1132), Peter of Poitiers (1087-1115), Ivo of Chartres (1090-1115), Ismido of Die (1098-1116), Geoffrey of Amiens (1104-1115), Odo of Cambrai (1105-1113), Hugh of Auxerre (1115-1136), and Peter of Tarentaise (1141-1174); all but two of these (Peter of Poitiers and Ismido of Die) had been monks. In the second half of the century, however, there

---

12. Marcel Pacaut, *Louis VII et les élections épiscopales dans la royaume de France* (Paris, 1957), pp. 111-12. Thomas Callahan, Jr., "The Renaissance of Monastic Bishops in England, 1135-1154," *Studia Monastica* 16 (1974), 55-67 (the only break in the steady decline in the number of English monastic bishops took place during the turbulent years of Stephen's reign). See also Constance B. Bouchard, "The Geographical, Social and Ecclesiastical Origins of the Bishops of Auxerre and Sens in the Central Middle Ages," *Church History* 46 (1977), 287-90.
13. Pierre Delooz, *Sociologie et canonisations* (Liège, 1969), pp. 350, 355.

were only two bishop-saints, Anthelm of Belley (1163–1177) and William of Bourges (1200–1209), both of whom had been monks.

There continued to be monk-bishops throughout the twelfth century, some of whom were sainted, even though both the proportion of monks and the proportion of saints in the French episcopacy decreased in the second half of the century. Bishop Thomas Becket of Canterbury (1162–1170), though he was chosen bishop for his administrative ability and was sainted more for his martyrdom than for his personal spirituality, assumed the monastic habit while in exile at Pontigny and adopted practices of mortifying the flesh.[14] But the decrease in the numbers of monks and saints among French bishops indicates that those selecting bishops were now often looking for qualities besides saintly immersion in the monastic virtues.

The Inescapable Duties of Office

Though Alain longed to escape the duties of his office for prayer and study in the cloister, his charters show that he was by no means an incompetent administrator. He settled quarrels, witnessed gifts, and reached favorable agreements with the counts. In fact, he was able to retain episcopal rights and property in the face of more direct threats to his temporal authority than a bishop of Auxerre had had to face since the beginning of the century. It may well be that Alain's troubles with the local nobility, especially the counts of Nevers, strengthened his determination to resign.

When Alain was consecrated, William III had been count for six years. Alain's biographer called William a serious adversary to the bishop, and Bernard described him as a lion ready to spring on the goods of the church, a man who did not walk in the ways of his father, William II, who had become a *conversus* at Chartreuse.[15] Alain, however, was able to reach an agreement with William III in 1157, spelling out the bishop's rights in the episcopal city of Cosne. In addition, the count promised Alain, as his father had promised Hugh of Mâcon in 1145, not to establish any new practices (*consuetudines*) at Auxerre or at the castles of Châteauneuf, St.-Sauveur, Cosne, Mailly, Bétry, and Lormes, which he held from the bishop—the last two castles were additions to those William II had agreed he held in fief from the bishop in 1145. Alain had been able to preserve and extend the bishop's rights in areas in which he was the count's secular superior.[16]

14. David Knowles, "Archbishop Thomas Becket: A Character Study," *The Historian and Character and Other Essays* (Cambridge, Eng., 1963), pp. 100–15.
15. *Gesta*, p. 421. Bernard of Clairvaux, Letter 280, PL 182:486–87.
16. Quantin 2.73, pp. 75–77.

Alain's biographer did not mention William IV, who succeeded his father in 1161 and proved to be a more difficult adversary of the church. William IV was above all considered the enemy of the abbey of Vézelay, in the diocese of Autun.[17] The quarrel between Vézelay and the counts of Nevers had continued intermittently since the time of Count Landric at the beginning of the eleventh century. The chronicler of Vézelay said that the sins of William II against the abbey were visited on his son when young Count Raynald died in the Holy Land. William III had encouraged the formation of a commune at Vézelay, against the wishes of the abbey, and he only retreated from his position in 1155 when he heard Louis VII was preparing an army against him; he sent Alain as his emissary to placate the king. William IV intensified the level of this continuing conflict. He cut off the abbey's supply of food when the monks would not pay certain *consuetudines* he demanded and then began carrying off their horses, cows, mules, and sheep. The archbishop of Sens unsuccessfully threatened the count with excommunication until Louis VII finally forced him to make peace in 1167, at which time William took the cross.

William IV was as hard an opponent for Alain as he was for the abbey of Vézelay. Alain appealed to the king for help against him, the only twelfth-century example of a bishop of Auxerre's asking a secular authority for assistance against a secular enemy. In 1164, Alain complained to Louis VII that the count had tried to dispose of ecclesiastical property according to his own will, had still not done the promised fealty for the lands he held from the bishop, and was on the point of seizing episcopal land at Varzy and Appoigny.[18] In a statement that would have scandalized his predecessors and successors alike, especially Humbaud and Hugh of Noyers, Alain said that his lands were the king's land and that only the king's men could protect them. Before Louis VII could respond, Count William appealed to Rome, attempting to prove that his father had never given fealty to the bishop and that the property he claimed was his, not the bishop's. The case was delegated by the pope to the former bishop of Langres and to the abbots of Clairvaux and Pontigny, but there was a slight delay in the beginning of their deliberations, as Alain first wanted to get the king's advice. The arbiters finally reached an amicable settlement, and William IV reconfirmed all the concessions his grandfather had made

17. For the details of the quarrel between Vézelay and the counts, see Hugh of Poitiers, *Historia Vizeliacensis monasterii* 2-4, ed. R. B. C. Huygens, *Monumenta Vizeliacensia*, Corpus Christianorum continuatio mediaevalis 42 (Turnhout, 1976), pp. 174-76, and the letter of Archbishop Hugh of Sens, PL 200:371-72.
18. PL 201:383-86.

before Bernard of Clairvaux in 1145. The count also reached compromises with Alain over the market and taxes of Auxerre and conceded that he could not demand military service from the bishop's men, but the agreement did not mention the lands seized at Varzy or Appoigny, nor even the fealty he owed the bishop; this fealty, however, was probably included under the reconfirmation of the charter of 1145, in which William II had done homage to the bishop for the castles of Châteauneuf, St.-Sauveur, Cosne, and Mailly.[19]

William IV stands out as Alain's chief opponent, but Alain also had trouble from other members of the local nobility. In 1153, Alain and the archbishop of Sens had to attempt to restrain a member of the petty nobility from building a castle on the land of the Cluniac house of La Charité. Another dispute is known only from a letter of Alexander III from about 1163. The pope wrote Alain that his case against a laymen who had seized some of his peasants should be argued on the basis of witnesses and documents, rather than submitted to a judicial duel. Canonists of the mid-twelfth century were insisting that such methods of proof as ordeals and dueling be replaced by reason, witnesses, and inspection of written documents.[20] Though the outcome of this particular case is unknown, it is indicative of the sorts of claims with which Alain had to deal.

Though Alain thus defended episcopal rights against the counts, he is not known to have bought any new episcopal property or to have rebuilt any episcopal buildings, as his successor was to do. He did give the cathedral some decorative hangings (*pallia*) and an elegantly written and illiminated copy of Gregory the Great's *Homilies on the Gospels*, according to his biographer, and he also announced that the cathedral canons might once again receive the revenues of the provostry for their common use, as had been established under Hugh of Montaigu, when the current provost died or otherwise vacated the office.[21] But here he was doing little more than reconfirming what his predecessors had already done, and in fact the provost Gui continued in that office until 1177, when he was elected archbishop of Sens.

In his treatment of diocesan affairs, Alain again attempted little that was new. Moreover, his charters indicate that other ecclesiastics and sometimes even secular authorities often witnessed gifts or settled the quarrels

---

19. *Gallia Christiana* 12:127-28, no. 40.
20. S. Loewenfeld, ed., *Epistolae pontificum Romanorum ineditae* (Leipzig, 1885), p. 113, no. 212. Quantin 2.148, p. 163. R. Van Caenegem, "The Law of Evidence in the Twelfth Century," *Proceedings of the Second International Congress of Medieval Canon Law*, p. 297.
21. *Gesta*, p. 420. Quantin 2.165, pp. 183-84.

which would have been handled by previous bishops of Auxerre. Alain frequently witnessed pious gifts and sales or rentals of land to local religious houses, especially Reigny,[22] but Pontigny usually had the archbishop witness its gifts now that the bishop of Auxerre was no longer a former abbot of Pontigny. Monasteries also began now to receive some of their gifts without ecclesiastical confirmation. For example, in 1164 and 1165, the count of Nevers issued the documents confirming gifts to St.-Marien and St.-Germain, and, in 1157, the count witnessed the confirmation by three brothers of their parents' gifts to Pontigny, gifts which had originally been made in 1146 before Bishop Hugh of Mâcon.[23]

Alain's own gifts to the local religious houses were often only confirmations or extensions of what his predecessors had already done. Thus, he assigned several cathedral prebends to St.-Eusèbe while confirming the agreement, between that house and the cathedral canons, which gave the canons of St.-Eusèbe the revenues for one year from each dead cathedral canon's prebend. He confirmed his predecessor's gifts to St.-Marien and added a parish church. He reconfirmed St.-Germain's right of election or presentation in the church of St.-Loup, and he had Pope Anastasius IV confirm in 1154 Eugenius III's regulation of the respective rights of the abbot of Cluny and the bishop of Auxerre over St.-Germain. He confirmed Hugh of Montaigu's establishment of canons regular in the church of St.-Amatre and submitted it to the direction of the house of St.-Satur near Bourges, a reformed house of Augustinian canons to which most Augustinian priories of the diocese of Bourges owed their direction.[24]

While thus attempting little that was new, Alain was sometimes even absent from ecclesiastical cases in which his predecessor would have been involved. Many quarrels between local religious houses were settled without him. For example in 1161 the archbishop reached a temporary settlement in the continuing quarrel between the nuns of St.-Julien of Auxerre and the count of Joigny over their respective rights in a woods near Joigny;

---

22. See especially the series of documents by which Reigny acquired, piecemeal, some land at Thorey, documents all issued by the bishop in 1162–63. Quantin 2.140, pp. 152–53; Arch. Yonne H 1627, nos. 91–93, 16, 112, 115.

23. For St.-Marien, see Quantin 2.152, p. 168. For St.-Germain, see Jean Lebeuf, *Mémoires concernant l'histoire civile et ecclésiastique d'Auxerre*, ed. and aug. Ambroise Challe and Maximilien Quantin, 4 (Auxerre, 1855), p. 47, no. 57. For Pontigny, see Quantin 2.76, pp. 81–82, and Quantin 1.258, p. 409.

24. For St.-Eusèbe, see Quantin 2.112, pp. 121–22, and Lebeuf, *Histoire d'Auxerre* 4:43–44, no. 49, and PL 188:1574. For St.-Marien, see Quantin 2.134, p. 145. For St.-Germain, see Quantin 1.361, pp. 519–21, and Quantin 2.166, pp. 184–85. For St.-Amatre, see Quantin 2.131, p. 142. For St.-Satur's position, see Guy Devailly, *Le Berry du Xe siècle au milieu du XIIIe* (Paris, 1973), p. 365.

the count of Nevers was a witness, but Alain was not. St.-Germain and the count of Nevers reached their own interim agreement, without the bishop, in a recurring quarrel over their respective rights in two small villages outside Auxerre. Three dignitaries of the cathedral chapter settled a quarrel between St.-Germain and the nobleman Stephen of Pierre-Pertuis; Alain merely witnessed the final agreement.[25] The pope himself found Alain remiss in bringing peace to the local churches. In 1156, Hadrian IV suggested rather forcibly to Alain that he should take care that Reigny obtained some property it had been given, in spite of rival claimants. On another occasion, Hadrian had to refer a case between one of the Auxerre cathedral canons and the provost of Lirey, near Troyes, to the bishop of Beauvais, after Alain proved unable to resolve the dispute.[26] Alain was not entirely remiss in carrying out papal mandates. In 1162, he with other Burgundian bishops and abbots settled a quarrel between the monastery of Cîteaux and the Hospitallers of Beaune.[27] Alain does not, however, seem to have taken any part in the decision of Thomas Becket to come to Pontigny in late 1164. Becket chose Pontigny because it was near the pope and settled there without any reference to the bishop in whose diocese the monastery was located.[28]

Alain's lack of complete involvement in the affairs of the churches of his diocese is especially marked because his episcopate fell at a time when the pope was playing an increasingly large role in the affairs of the local churches in Auxerre and indeed in all of France. The popes Hadrian IV and Alexander III confirmed the possessions of Pontigny and St.-Marien while Alain was bishop without any reference to him.[29] Alain referred many of his own administrative acts to the pope for confirmation, for example his gift of several chapter prebends to St.-Eusèbe. The king, too, as well as the count, began for the first time to play an important part in diocesan affairs. Louis VII carried out a complicated series of exchanges and transfers with St.-Marien in 1163-64 in order to obtain the land to found a new free city just outside Sens, and the bishop did not appear in any of the documents.[30] Of course, Alain's personality was not alone responsible for the more frequent presence of other ecclesiastical or secu-

---

25. Quantin 2.121, 89, 120, 147, pp. 130-31, 96-97, 128-30, 162-63. Quantin 1.365, pp. 524-25.
26. Quantin 1.380, p. 545. Hadrian IV, Letter 163, PL 188:1541-42.
27. J. Marilier, ed., *Chartes et documents concernant l'abbaye de Cîteaux* (Rome, 1961), pp. 127-30, nos. 160, 163.
28. Herbert of Bosham, *Vita S. Thomae* 4.12, RS 67, 3:357.
29. Quantin 1.384, pp. 549-50. Quantin 2.127, pp. 136-38.
30. Quantin 2.133, 135, 145, 151, pp. 143-44, 146, 161, 167.

lar figures in local affairs, for something similar was happening all over France. The pope in the second half of the twelfth century frequently adjudicated cases which had not already passed through the local bishop's hands. The upper nobility and the king were trying to establish jurisdictional competence over all the men of their lands, including the clergy.[31] The change was more marked at Auxerre only because king and pope became more concerned with the details of ecclesiastical administration at the local level at a time when the bishop was a man who considered his administrative duties a heavy burden.

There is, nevertheless, evidence that Alain did honestly attempt to carry out his administrative duties as bishop, especially those involving the welfare of the local religious houses. Though the pope, the archbishop, and the count witnessed gifts to local houses and confirmed their possessions, Alain's charters in the archives of the local houses greatly outnumber those of anyone else for the years that he was bishop. Alain may not have shown an ability to make peace or a desire to initiate new programs or major reforms, but the memory of his episcopate that his biographer recorded was that he was helpful to many of the churches of Auxerre, "pleasing both God and man."[32]

Conclusions

For Alain, the chief attribute of a religious man was monastic withdrawal combined with contemplation and study. This attitude reflected the presupposition of twelfth-century monastic culture that prayer and literary studies together made the soul thirst for God and indicated the direction of its fulfillment;[33] it does not, however, seem to have reflected the ideas on the duties of a worthy bishop held by the contemporary secular clergy. In contrast with what he believed a religious man should do, Alain apparently believed that the chief responsibility for a bishop was to defend his church's temporal rights and possessions as best he could. In spite of the general ecclesiastical belief that a bishop should not leave his see and Bernard's specific pronouncements to this effect, Alain spent much of his episcopate trying to resign. He did not want to continue in an office whose responsibilities he found incompatible with the religious life.

Ecclesiastical administration had become much more complex in the second half of the twelfth century than it had been earlier in the century.

---

31. Lemarignier, Gaudemet, and Mollat, *Institutions ecclésiastiques*, pp. 262–63, 273–74.
32. *Gesta*, p. 420; cf. 2 Cor. 8.21.
33. Leclercq, *Love of Learning*, pp. 309–39.

Episcopal decisions were expected to conform to a more systematic body of law with the spread of Gratian's *Decretum*. The existence of agreements between bishops and the local authorities detailing their specific rights made it necessary for the bishops to defend these prerogatives if the local nobility began to encroach upon them. The archbishop and the pope appeared more frequently in local diocesan affairs, and cases were often appealed to them from the bishop's court. Although France saw no confrontations between secular and ecclesiastical justice as dramatic as the conflict in England between King Henry II and Archbishop Thomas Becket over "criminous clerks," the French king also attempted to extend his jurisdiction, in spite of ecclesiastical opposition. The increase in the amount and complexity of episcopal business required that the bishop give a great deal of attention to administration. This was the *vita activa* which Alain resigned to return to the cloister and the *vita contemplativa*. The monastic life Alain preferred was followed by fewer French bishops after the middle of the twelfth century, as the number of bishops from the regular clergy shrank. When Alain abdicated, the chapter elected, without hesitation or disagreement, a man who had many years of administrative experience as archdeacon and provost of Sens.

WILLIAM OF TOUCY
AND EPISCOPAL AUTHORITY

The man whom the Auxerre cathedral canons elected to succeed Alain appears from his biography and his documents to have been a man outstanding in administrative ability. William of Toucy (1167–1181) cared for the rights of local religious houses even when these houses did not protect their rights themselves, and he expanded episcopal property to a degree unprecedented among twelfth-century bishops of Auxerre. The first bishop of Auxerre from the secular clergy in fifty years, he preferred the company of both clerics and laymen to a life of withdrawal and prayer, and he maintained a large and expensive household. His biographer, Fromond, a commensal of the bishop and the first twelfth-century biographer of the bishops of Auxerre whose name is known, described William as loved by all the clergy and laymen of the diocese, eventually even by his enemies.

Little is known about Fromond other than his name. He appears in none of the bishop's charters, although according to the biography he often accompanied William on his trips around the diocese. In his work he gave precedence to the bishop's struggles against the counts and his extensive renovations of episcopal property. Scattered throughout the biography are comments that the bishop's deeds demonstrated his virtuous nature. After a short initial section on William's family and election, followed by 100 words on the bishop's attention to liturgical observance, Fromond devoted a 1200-word passage to the bishop's temporal administration, starting with an account of the "tribulations and anguish" brought on by the counts, continuing with the bishop's triumphs, and finally giving a list of all the property William acquired from the count and from others and how he improved it. The biographer then devoted a 400-word section to the bishop's pastoral activities and a 450-word section to the repairs he made to the cathedral and the gifts he made to local churches. The latter section was prefaced with the comment, "He did many other things worth recording, but let us pass over them and now turn to what he did for his own church and other churches." Fromond thus made a sharp distinction in the structure of his work between care for episcopal goods and care for the local churches, and he put care for episcopal goods first. The final 1200 words of the biography are an account of the long illness that ended in William's death. The theme of death, the point at which one must show love of one's brother and obedience to God, reappears throughout the biography.

William was elected with a rapidity that suggests that he had displayed characteristics in his years as archdeacon of Sens that the Auxerre chapter now considered highly desirable in a bishop. William came originally from the petty nobility of the Auxerrois, the *Narbonnia* family of Toucy. This family, which should not be confused with the family of the lords of Toucy, was related by marriage with the lords of Seignelay and Pierre-Pertuis, two of the more powerful families of the region. The *Narbonnia* family provided a number of ecclesiastics for the churches of Sens and Auxerre during the twelfth century. William's older brother Hugh was archbishop of Sens (1143–1168) and made his two younger brothers, William and Hervé, archdeacon and provost of the Sens chapter at least as early as 1146.[1] After Hervé died around 1160, William filled both offices, and less than a year before Alain's resignation, William was elected treasurer of the Auxerre cathedral chapter. After he became bishop, he was succeeded as archdeacon of Sens by a certain Hugh, one of his nephews, who later built William's tomb at Auxerre.[2]

When Archbishop Hugh of Toucy allowed Alain to resign in 1167, in direct contravention of several previous papal refusals, he probably did so knowing that the Auxerre chapter would promptly elect his brother William. The rapidity and apparent unanimity with which the canons did so, however, would indicate a real desire for William, a man of undoubted ability, whom they knew well. Because of the indisputable canonical correctness of the process of the election, Alexander III permitted Hugh to consecrate William, even though he severely reprimanded the archbishop.

Defense and Improvement of Ecclesiastical Property

Fromond indicated that the ability which the canons saw in William was demonstrated especially in his strong stand against the counts of Nevers. William IV, with whom Alain had had so much difficulty, went to the Holy Land the same year Alain resigned and died there shortly afterwards. As he left no children, his younger brother Gui succeeded him as count. After burying his brother in the Holy Land, Gui returned with heavy debts weighing on him. Fromond said that he was "led astray by perverse counsel" and tried to set aside all the ancient customary rights and

1. Quantin 1.263, p. 416.
2. Robert of St.-Marien, p. 239. Arch. Yonne G 1849. *Gesta*, p. 431.

dues of Auxerre (*antiqui consuetudines*) to establish new ones favorable to himself.[3] At this time, grape-growing had become very profitable for places like Auxerre, located on a river providing good transportation, because of the increasing demand for wine in the towns of northern France.[4] Looking for profit, Gui turned first to the vineyards of Auxerre.

Gui took all the winepresses of the city under his jurisdiction, so that none of them could be operated unless he were paid a fee. According to his biographer, William resisted this presumption so "manfully" (*viriliter*) that no cleric or townsman ever had to pay the fee. Not discouraged, Gui next persuaded the local churches to let him set his own men to gather and keep the tithes of their vineyards, as they were being harvested. Fromond related that William intervened promptly, determined to protect the churches' rights, even when they made no attempt to protect them themselves. The method by which William forced Gui to give up the grape presses is not recorded, but he used the force of interdict and a papal bull in making the count restore tithes to the churches.[5]

But Gui was not yet daunted. Fromond recorded that after his efforts to earn money from local wine production failed, he next attempted to establish a commune at Auxerre. Communes, associations for mutual protection and self-government, were being formed in a number of northern and southern French towns and villages during the twelfth century. A commune needed to be recognized by an existing authority to become an authority in itself, and it could often find a lord willing to do so, since he could expect in return a share of the town's profits.[6] It is not clear whether Gui originated the idea of a commune at Auxerre or whether the townspeople had already been attempting to establish one, but William immediately opposed it. Most French bishops considered the formation of a commune to be an act of hostility to their authority, since communes generally claimed rights to exercise justice that had formerly been exercised by the bishop and his officials. William had already witnessed the episcopal suppression of one commune, at Sens in 1146–47, and he would not tolerate a commune in his diocese.[7]

---

3. *Gesta*, p. 422.
4. Roger Dion, *Histoire de la vigne et du vin en France des origines au XIXe siècle* (Paris, 1959), pp. 49, 201, 245.
5. *Gesta*, pp. 422–23.
6. Pierre Michaud-Quantin, *Universitas: Expressions du mouvement communautaire dans le moyen-âge latin* (Paris, 1970), p. 163. Georges Duby, *Guerriers et paysans, VII–XIIe siècle: Premier essor de l'économie européenne* (Paris, 1973), p. 276.
7. Michaud-Quantin, *Universitas*, p. 241. Jean-François Lemarignier, Jean Gaudemet, and Guillaume Mollat, *Institutions ecclésiastiques*, Histoire des institutions françaises

Fromond gave a great deal of detail on the commune, which he presented as an example both of the dangers William faced and of his strength and ability in overcoming them. Gui had obtained the king's permission for the commune, and William incurred royal wrath when he tried to end it; Fromond stated that Louis VII believed that "all cities in which a commune was established were his own."[8] Of course only those communes which the king established himself were in fact his, but Fromond's comment indicates the increasing general influence of the king in this region removed from Paris and the biographer's specific fear that the king could become a real threat to the bishop's authority in local secular affairs. But William persisted, "not without great danger and expense." As Gui had found it useful to gain the king's support in establishing the commune, William found it necessary to gain the king's support to end it. He showed the king the charter signed by William II in 1145, reconfirmed by Gui's father William III and brother William IV, in which the count agreed that no changes or new customs should be established at Auxerre without the bishop's express consent. On the basis of these documents, and a large sum of money paid to the king and his men, Fromond said that William finally obtained a royal privilege in 1173 ending the commune and establishing that none be set up in the future without the bishop's consent. In spite of any anger toward William on the king's part, Fromond said that Louis continued to consider him "one of the best bishops in the realm."[9] Though there is no evidence that the king actually expressed such a sentiment, Fromond was here indicating that William was able to triumph against his secular enemies while preserving their friendship.

Not long after William obtained the royal privilege ending the commune at Auxerre, Gui fell seriously ill, which Fromond said was an act of "divine mercy" as it put an end to the count's persecution of churches. For him, God was clearly on the bishop's side when he resisted the count. Fromond did not despair of the count's soul, however, and in fact recorded that William saved it. Although William lifted the excommunication that he had laid on the count—he was much quicker to use the weapon of excommunication than his predecessors had been—the count was still under a sentence of excommunication laid on him by the bishops

au moyen âge 3 (Paris, 1962), p. 274. Albert Vermeesch, *Essai sur les origines et la signification de la commune dans le Nord de la France (XIe et XIIe siècles)* (Huele, Belgium, 1966), p. 125.

8. *Gesta*, p. 423: ". . . [Ludovicus] reputans civitates omnes suas esse in quibus communie essent."

9. Ibid., pp. 423, 428. *Gallia Christiana* 12:135, no. 50.

of Nevers and Autun for reopening his brother's quarrels with Vézelay. When the count seemed to be dying, Fromond recorded that the great barons (*proceres*) and the bishops of Burgundy sought a bishop to absolve him. As neither the bishop of Nevers nor the bishop of Autun cared to or dared to, William, "moved by piety and faith" according to his biographer, said that he would always be ashamed if he let such a man as the count die excommunicate. Putting the burden of responsibility for the count's deeds at Vézelay on his own shoulders and on those of the barons, William absolved Gui, winning the admiration and love not only of the barons but, according to Fromond, of Gui himself, who henceforth considered William "not as his bishop or his lord but as his father." The bishop Fromond portrayed not only won his battles but was reconciled with his enemies. For this deathbed absolution, according to Fromond and contemporary charters, William received a gift of about 30 peasant families at Varzy from Gui's mother and 20 pounds in annual revenue to establish an altar in the cathedral of Auxerre where daily mass would be said for the soul of Gui and all his ancestors. Gui himself, lingering a little longer, added to this a gift of all the men he had at La-Chapelle-St.-André, five kilometers from Varzy.[10]

Following Gui's death in 1176, there was what Fromond described as a "rapid turnover" in counts of Nevers. As Gui's children were very young, the three counties of Auxerre, Nevers, and Tonnerre were ruled by his widow, the Countess Mathilda, granddaughter of Duke Hugh II of Burgundy. Mathilda had already been married once before, to Odo of Issoudun, and had borne him an heir; after Gui's death, she promptly married Peter of Flanders, who shortly died, and then around 1182 Robert of Dreux, from whom she was soon forced to separate on grounds of consanguinuity. Her third and fourth husbands styled themselves counts of Nevers, but neither gave the bishop of Auxerre any trouble.[11]

Though the count of Nevers was always William's chief adversary. Fromond recorded that William also had quarrels with other members of the local nobility. He became involved in a dispute over the boundary between some episcopal land and the land of Stephen of Pierre-Pertuis, a powerful man who was his own blood relative. William took the case to the archbishop of Sens (who was no longer his brother), putting "justice

---

10. *Gesta*, pp. 422–24. *Gallia Christiana* 12:135–36, no. 51.
11. Robert of St.-Marien, p. 244. J. Marilier, ed., *Chartes et documents concernant l'abbaye de Cîteaux* (Paris, 1961), pp. 122–23, 187, 196–97, nos. 150, 237, 248. *Gallia Christiana* 4:92, no. 58. Robert of St.-Michel, *Chronica*, PL 160:523–24. *Cartulaire du prieuré de Jully-les-Nonnains*, ed. Ernest Petit, *Bulletin de la Société des sciences historiques et naturelles de l'Yonne* 34 (1880), 273.

before propinquity" in his biographer's words, and obtained a settlement in his favor. So that there would be no question in the future about the extent of episcopal lands, William erected a cross on the boundary between Stephen's lands and his own. When Narjod, lord of Toucy, planned to build a tower at the episcopal city of Toucy, William paid him 140 pounds for its construction, on the condition that whenever the bishop or his successors should wish to have the use of the tower, Narjod and his successors would yield it to him; Fromond specified that this agreement would be renewed by each new lord of Toucy. Although Hervé, lord of Donzy, long refused to do homage to the bishop for the episcopal city of Gien, William finally extracted this homage from Hervé on his deathbed; Fromond said that this assured that "his church lost none of its rights." In all of these instances, Fromond showed William as firmly settling his quarrels with the local nobility and establishing that they should not recur under his successors.[12]

Besides protecting his rights and his land, William made many purchases of additional land and improved what he already had. Although Fromond said that the things William did were too numerous for him to describe in full, he still gave many details. The bishops had long had a castle at Varzy though little else. Now that he had obtained a number of men there from the count and his mother, William bought out a layman's share in the castellany, obtained a number of vineyards, meadows, and buildings there, and acquired more men at Corvol, seven kilometers to the south. Closer to Auxerre, William walled the episcopal city of Gy-l'Evêque (9 kilometers south of Auxerre), built houses and an oven, had vineyards planted, and acquired more men. At Charbuy (8 kilometers northwest of Auxerre), he bought all of one knight's possessions and acquired meadows and forest land. At the episcopal city of Appoigny (10 kilometers north of Auxerre), he bought meadows, vineyards, woods, and arable fields from several knights. At Toucy, as well as paying for the construction of a tower, he built a new episcopal palace and cellar and bought several meadows and fields. At the episcopal city of Cosne (65 kilometers southwest of Auxerre), he bought a grange with its oxen, plow, meadows, and fields. At Auxerre itself, he bought the right to receive 20 pounds annually from the convent of St.-Julien, bought and tore down some houses that had crowded inconveniently close to the episcopal palace, made a walled courtyard for the palace, and bought other pieces of property throughout the city that Fromond found too numerous to mention.[13]

12. *Gesta*, pp. 424–25.
13. Ibid.

All the purchases recorded in the biography were, according to Fromond, "worthy of memory" (*memoria digna*). He could easily have listed many more, he said, except that he might have appeared tedious (*fastidiosus*). The large number of details which he did give indicate that William expanded episcopal property in a way that none of his predecessors had done since Humbaud. Purchase, involving large sums of money, the amount of which Fromond usually recorded carefully, was important as it had not been before. William found himself at the head of the church of Auxerre when France entered what Duby has called a new economic phase, one in which the use of money increased, prices rose, and land was sold more often than it was given.[14] Yet in responding to these changes, William was by no means abandoning the precedent of his predecessors. For the most part, he bought land, improved it, and built houses where his predecessors had already been active. The towns of Varzy, Gy-l'Evêque, Appoigny, Toucy, Cosne, and of course Auxerre itself had all contained property belonging to the bishops of Auxerre since long before the days of bishop Humbaud. The land William acquired and the improvements he made would in turn be the basis of further improvements by his successors.

In a passage separated from this section on the bishop's improvements to his temporal property, Fromond gave a description of the renovations William "piously and mercifully" carried out in the cathedral of St. Stephen. The roof had had no work done on it since Humbaud's time, sixty years earlier, but William now gave the cathedral a new stone arch and all new tiles. He also put steeples with stained glass at either end of the roof and rebuilt the entire upper portion of one tower. To decorate the re-roofed cathedral, Fromond recorded, William gave the church a fine hanging (*pallium*) and a silver ewer for holding the holy water. At the time he made his testament, he gave in addition a silver ciborium in which to put the Body of the Lord and several basins, vestments, and books for use in the celebration of the Mass. William also rededicated several altars within the cathedral. Fromond described how he used the revenues he had received in return for a daily mass for Count Gui's soul to establish several clerks serving the newly dedicated altar of St. Gilles the Confessor. In addition, in both the church itself and in the crypts below, he established altars to St. John the Evangelist, St. Paul, St. Mary Magdalene, St. Andrew the

---

14. Georges Duby dates this change for northern France to either 1160 (*La société aux XIe et XIIe siècles dans la région mâconnaise*, 2nd ed. [Paris, 1971], pp. 360-65), or 1180 (*Guerriers et paysans*, p. 285). Either of these dates will do for Auxerre, as William's pontificate, in which the change first became apparent, fell between them.

Apostle, St. Laurent the Martyr, St. Germain, and Sts. Cyricus and Julitta; the last two were martyrs under Diocletian whose relics were brought from Antioch to Auxerre in the fifth century by the sainted bishop Amatre. William established that the clerks of Notre-Dame-la-Cité would say a daily mass for his own soul and for Fromond's at the new altar of Mary Magdalene.[15] The chronicler Robert of St.-Marien, who began to write about the time of William's death, devoted only a short section of his work to William, but he like Fromond praised the bishop's pious attention to the cathedral altars.

Fromond followed this account of William's improvements to the cathedral with a record of his generosity to the local houses. He listed in detail the parish churches which the bishop gave to the monasteries of Notre-Dame-la-Dehors (the priory of St.-Marien), St.-Pierre, St.-Laurent of Cosne, and Crisenon. The documents indicate that William also reconfirmed his predecessors' gifts to St.-Marien, added the gift of a millrace, and confirmed his chapter's gift of the bridge over the millrace. In addition, with the assent of Alexander III, he transformed the Augustinian priory of St.-Pierre into an abbey, a change that gave added prestige to the house, even if it had little effect on the lives of the brothers. Fromond said that the bishop gave so many benefices of this kind that, after his death, there was not a conventual house in the diocese that did not solemnly celebrate his anniversary.[16] William was a generous benefactor of local churches, as his biographer described him, and his documents show that he often helped arbitrate quarrels between the local nobility and diocesan houses, especially St.-Germain and Reigny.[17]

This effective administrator was also, according to his biographer, concerned with ecclesiastical affairs beyond the border of his diocese. Fromond credited William, when still archdeacon of Sens, with making the decision to support Alexander III against the emperor's candidate after the papal election of 1159, a decision, he said, that influenced the other French bishops and led to the eventual end of the schism. He also recorded that William attended Alexander's ecumenical council, Lateran III, in 1179. This council, in addition to concluding the schism and ordaining the method by which popes would henceforth be elected, gave in twenty-seven

15. *Gesta*, pp. 427–30.
16. Ibid., pp. 427–28. For William's gifts to St.-Marien, see Quantin 2.259, pp. 278–79 and Arch. Yonne H 1233. For the transformation of St.-Pierre into an abbey, see Quantin 2.231, pp. 248–49.
17. For St.-Germain, see Quantin 2.190, pp. 207–08, and Bibl. Auxerre, Cart. St.-Germain, fol. 56v, no. 8. For Reigny, see Quantin 2.272, pp. 291–92, and Arch. Yonne H 1627, nos. 4 and 101.

long and detailed canons decrees on such matters as the sacerdotal grade necessary for various capitular offices, the manner of receiving bishops when they made tours of diocesan visitation, the establishment of a *magister* and a school in every cathedral, and the episcopal obligation to oppose heresy. Topics such as marriage of the clergy, tournaments, and the protection of Crusaders' possessions, which had formed a major part of the decrees of Lateran I and II, were moved toward the end of the canons and condensed, in favor of numerous details on how a bishop should administer his diocese.[18]

The detailed canons of this council were symptomatic of the growing complexity of ecclesiastical affairs and the growing importance of papal decisions at the local level in the later twelfth century. Although the king and the archbishop on occasion also influenced diocesan affairs, their role was small compared to the pope's. At Auxerre, the king drew up the terms of an agreement between the count and the cathedral chapter and confirmed the possessions of Pontigny in 1177 as well as first supporting and then suppressing the commune.[19] Since Archbishop William of Champagne, who succeeded Hugh of Toucy in the see of Sens in 1168, was made papal legate, his intermittent presence in the affairs of the Auxerrois represented papal interests as well as his own.

Alexander III was a lawyer, as were all notable popes throughout the rest of the twelfth and thirteenth centuries; legalistic tendencies were thus strong in his decrees. The pope and his councils were establishing norms for many details of diocesan administration that had been left to individual bishops earlier in the century. Ecclesiastical courts and canon law were becoming much more centralized. At Auxerre, Alexander personally confirmed the elevation of St.-Pierre into an abbey in 1174, confirmed in 1173 the possessions of St.-Marien and granted the canons the right to present candidates for the office of parish priest in those parish churches under their patronage, and delegated to William and the bishop of Troyes a quarrel appealed to the Roman curia by the bishop of Autun. William readily carried out this charge, although Alain had been unable to settle one quarrel known to have been delegated to him by the pope.[20]

Fromond strongly approved of William's administrative ability and called him "the first among the bishops of Auxerre."[21] The biography and

18. *Gesta*, pp. 421, 428. Raymonde Foreville, *Latran I, II, III et Latran IV* (Paris, 1965), pp. 134–58, 389. Hefele-Leclercq, *Histoire des conciles*, 5, 2:1086–1112.
19. Quantin 2.227, pp. 243–44. Achille Luchaire, *Etudes sur les actes de Louis VII* (Paris, 1885), p. 324, no. 717.
20. Quantin 2.127, p. 138. Alexander III, Letter 952, PL 200:834.
21. *Gesta*, p. 431.

the documents give a similar picture of a vigorous bishop who defended his rights, expanded and improved his property, protected the local churches, participated in councils, and tried to save a count's sinful soul. In this last case, Fromond made it clear that he saw no separation between vigorous (and often secularly oriented) administration and good pastoral care.

The Changing Meaning of Humility

William was not a monk, and Fromond did not describe him as emulating one. Rather than using monastic terms to describe his subject's spirituality, as had earlier biographers at Auxerre, he described William's virtues as evident in his care for the souls committed to him and in his propagation of liturgical observance. The differences between Fromond's views on episcopal spirituality and those of earlier biographers are especially clear in the way in which Fromond described his subject's "humility."

He used the word *humilis* with some frequency in his biography of William, but he gave it a different meaning than had the three preceding biographers. They had all equated humility with poverty and withdrawal, but Fromond did not describe his subject as having these characteristics. Instead, he said approvingly that William had gained a reputation as archdeacon of Sens for his lavish hospitality and his large and expensive household (*familia*) of servants and retainers. There were only a few traces in the biography of actions that previous biographers would have called signs of humility: William asking to be buried in the vilest sacerdotal vestment that could be found, or considering himself to have left secular fame and praise, if not secular display, when he became bishop.[22] Fromond described these incidents in passing and did not call them signs of humility.

What he did call humility was demonstrated not in a simple monastic life but rather in actions more in keeping with vigorous action *in* the world, particularly firm administration and liberal generosity. Fromond used the term "humility" as close in meaning to "nobility"; he said that William's parents, noble and outstanding for their possessions and their blood, were made even more noble (*nobiliores*) by having as sons an archbishop of Sens and a bishop of Auxerre.[23] All the incidents which Fromond described as demonstrating William's humility involved either a vigorous defense of his church's rights or a paternalistic sympathy for the needs of the poor. In describing how William resisted the count, he said that the bishop, as a "humble" man, won a decision from the pope to be sure that neither the cathedral nor any other church of Auxerre should

22. Ibid., pp. 421–22.
23. Ibid., p. 421.

have anything happen to its detriment. A little later in the biography, Fromond said that he would give other examples of William's "humility," and then related two incidents in which William agreed to give communion to a dying villager.[24] Like earlier biographers, Fromond labeled as humility those characteristics he found most important in a bishop, but he was describing different characteristics. He used standard terminology to describe someone whom he considered an excellent bishop, but by attaching novel connotations to the term humility he was able to express a concept very different from those of the biographers who had described monastic bishops.

This change was by no means merely local. Some of Fromond's contemporaries also used the term *humilitas* with an altered meaning. Alain of Lille, writing a few years earlier, had emphasized the "natural" virtues to the point that he reduced the sense of humility to simple fortitude against tribulations. The schools where the pagan philosophers were being read more and more at the end of the twelfth century were relegating the evangelical virtues, including humility in the sense that biographers at Auxerre had used it since the time of Hugh of Montaigu, to a vague upper realm.[25]

When Fromond described humility as expressed in his bishop's sympathy for the poor, it was generally linked to a love of the liturgy. For example, he told of two "miraculous" cures that William performed, in each case because he was "humble" enough to take the sacraments where needed, even into the vilest hut. On one occasion, as William was passing through a poor village, Fromond related that a woman ran up to him crying, "Have mercy on me, thou son of David," as the Canaanite woman had called to Jesus for help for her daughter (Matt. 15.22). Her husband was dying, and the bishop agreed to give the benediction, though this task would normally have fallen to the local parish priest. (The biographer's allusion to the Canaanite woman is of interest here, since Jesus at first refused to hear her petition on the grounds that the Canaanites were not included in his ministry. In ministering to the poor, William was clearly going beyond the ordinary practice of a bishop.) Although Fromond was not present on this occasion, he said that he heard later that the dying man had been restored to life, and that the woman considered it a miracle worked by God through the bishop.

Fromond was present on another occasion when William, on his way to dedicate a chapel, delayed his trip in order to hear the confession of a

---

24. Ibid., pp. 422, 425: ". . . vir pius et humilis ita sedare studuit quid nec sua, nec alie sibi subdite ecclesie de juris sui integritate aliquid detrimenti omnino senserunt."

25. M.-D. Chenu, *La théologie au douzième siècle* (Paris, 1957), p. 36.

dying boy and to give him communion. In the biographer's words, "not the filth, not the odors, nor the vileness of the bed" kept William from administering the viaticum with his own hand. Although the boy died almost immediately, Fromond described this incident as nearly identical with the earlier miraculous healing; he said that the bishop was sure the boy was now blessed and indicated that saving the boy's soul was as much a sign of divine favor as saving the man's life on the earlier occasion. William, he said, was glad that he had preferred the "Lord's work" of administering final rites to hurrying to keep an appointment at the chapel.[26] He used the term *opus Domini* to mean bringing the liturgy to his parishioners, again a different meaning of the term than the monastic *opus Dei* of liturgical celebration within the cloister. Fromond here distinguished between ecclesiastical administration—dedicating a chapel—and the "Lord's work" of saving souls, but he did not carry the distinction further.

Fromond's inclusion of these two miracles was an indication that the virtues he described in William were the virtues that God rewarded in a bishop. For the biographer, true spirituality was expressed in ritual observance. He further described William as establishing that the summer feast of St. Martin be celebrated solemnly, ringing the big bells. He said that the bishop celebrated Mass daily unless "necessity" intervened, regularly sang psalms while riding through the diocese on business, and could not fall asleep without the music of the psalms in his ears.[27] The bishop's love for the liturgy and concern for those around him was said to have lasted until his death.

The final third of the biography is devoted to the piety and virtue that William showed in the last four months of his life. Fromond described how William, while wasting toward the grave, prepared for an orderly transition to his successor. He made his testament before the bishop of Nevers, the abbot of Vézelay, who was his cousin, and the cathedral canons. He sold his possessions to pay his debts and to make gifts to establish the observance of his anniversary. He urged the canons not to let any "pernicious schism" keep them from the prompt election of his successor, but rather to ask the king at once for the *licentia eligendi* (see above, Chapter IV) and to choose a man who was upright, learned, and affable. In his final months, Fromond said that William observed the Advent fast in spite of his weakened condition, continued to sing psalms with the brothers, and asked his visitors to pray that he have a good death rather than pray that he recover. When he

26. *Gesta*, pp. 425–26.
27. Ibid., pp. 422, 428.

finally died, there was wailing and lamenting throughout the city, but his own face showed "blessed" stillness, as if he were only sleeping.[28]

Fromond described William's death as the culmination of an undoubtedly holy life. He wrote at a time when many thinkers within the church were putting less stress than had those a generation earlier on a life of monastic poverty and humility as the authentic religious life.[29] The voluntary adoption of poverty was even viewed on occasion with suspicion, because of the importance given to it by the increasingly numerous heretical groups. Indeed, a desire for poverty and a humble life, coupled with preaching not approved by the organized church, was a predominant feature of twelfth-century heresy. Though religious enthusiasts within the orthodox church continued to embrace poverty, much of the church organization was moving in another direction. When poverty went beyond personal asceticism to become a religious ideal and goal, the organized church felt its integrity threatened. An example of this sort of threat was Arnold of Brescia, who wanted clerics, including monks and bishops, to give up all their property to laymen; he led groups practicing a life of austerity as a more direct way to God than through organized religion, and, after fifteen years of papal condemnation, he was burned as a heretic in 1155.[30] Otto of Freising, recognizing the differences between the *humiliatio* of the church in its early centuries and its contemporary *exaltatio*, questioned whether the former might be better, but concluded that the latter was certainly more pleasant.[31] The term *ecclesia primitiva*, which in the eleventh and early twelfth centuries had been used to mean the ideal life of poverty and common property to which ecclesiastical corporations should be reformed, was, by the middle of the twelfth century, sometimes treated by canonists with derision, as an expression of

---

28. Ibid., pp. 428–31.
29. Herbert Grundmann, *Religiöse Bewegungen im Mittelalter*, 2nd ed. (Hildesheim, 1961), p. 15. Chenu, *La théologie au douzième siècle*, p. 255. Glenn Olsen, "The Idea of the *Ecclesia Primitiva* in the Writings of the Twelfth-Century Canonists," *Traditio* 25 (1969), 64–71. Jean Leclercq, "The Monastic Crisis of the Eleventh and Twelfth Centuries," in *Cluniac Monasticism in the Central Middle Ages*, ed. Noreen Hunt (London, 1971), p. 231. Christopher Brooke, "Heresy and Religious Sentiment," *Medieval Church and Society* (London, 1971), p. 152.
30. Otto of Freising, *Gesta Friderici I Imperatoris* 1.28 and 2.28, ed. George Waitz (1912), Scriptores Rerum Germanicarum in Usum Scholarum, pp. 35–36, 106–07. Augustin Fliche, *Du premier concile du Latran à l'avènement d'Innocent III (1123–1198)*, Histoire de l'église depuis les origines jusqu'à nos jours 9 (Paris, 1946), pp. 99–102. André Vauchez, *La spiritualité du moyen age occidental, VIIIe–XIIe siècles* (Paris, 1975), p. 119.
31. Otto of Freising, *Chronica sive Historia de duabus civitatibus* 4.prol., ed. Adolf Hofmeister (1912), Scriptores Rerum Germanicarum in Usum Scholarum, p. 183.

crude practices away from which the church had evolved.[32] Even the Cistercian Order, the chief example of a monastic life of poverty and humility within the twelfth-century church, began within months of Bernard's death in 1153 to modify his strict emphasis on poverty in order to allow greater wealth, including previously forbidden regular incomes from outside sources.

In deemphasizing monastic poverty and humility as the ideals toward which all ecclesiastics should strive, the organized church instead made care of souls and preaching (when done by a properly authorized priest) the center of the ideal religious life.[33] Alain of Lille put preaching at the top of the ladder of religious perfection, rather than personal and individual striving for salvation. The *vita apostolica*, when still presented as a model for religious life, meant preaching to the world as Jesus and his disciples had done, rather than praying for the world within the cloister. Action and decision began to be considered by some a more important aspect of the spiritual life than obedience and conformity within a monastery. Many ecclesiastics had come to believe that error must be overcome with preaching or even with force, rather than simply by setting a moral example. This belief was the impetus for the new orders of the later twelfth and early thirteenth centuries.[34] Fromond's biography, in which he described William as a holy man without giving him any of the monastic attributes that earlier biographers had used as examples of episcopal virtue, was thus part of the changing understanding of spirituality in the French church in the later twelfth century.

Conclusions

Unlike Alain, Fromond saw no conflict between living a holy life and fulfilling the duties of a bishop. In fact, his use of biblical allusions contained the implication that William was a very holy man, even Christlike. He had the wife of the dying villager address William as "Son of David." He had William take the burden of the count's sins on his own shoulders in a passage reminiscent of the Suffering Servant. Just before his

32. Olsen, "The Idea of the *Ecclesia Primitiva*," pp. 64–71.
33. Chenu, *La théologie au douzième siècle*, pp. 243, 253–58. Yves Congar, "Modèle monastique et modèle sacerdotal en Occident de Grégoire VII (1073–1085) à Innocent III (1198)," in *Etudes de civilisation médiévale (IXe-XIIe siècles): Mélanges offerts à Edmond-René Labande* (Poitiers, 1974), p. 156. See also Barbara H. Rosenwein and Lester K. Little, "Social Meaning in the Monastic and Mendicant Spiritualities," *Past and Present* 63 (1974), 21–22.
34. Giles Constable, "Twelfth-Century Spirituality and the Late Middle Ages," *Medieval and Renaissance Studies* 5 (1969), 40–41. Chenu, *La théologie au douzième siècle*, pp. 227–29, 257–58.

death, Fromond recorded that William told the canons, "Peace I leave with you; my peace I give to you," using the same words Jesus had used to comfort his disciples shortly before the Crucifixion (John 15.27). Fromond found holiness in liturgical observance, defense of the rights of local churches and his own, and sympathy for the poor, all of which he called demonstrations of William's "humility."

In this biography, not only were spirituality and administrative ability compatible, they were almost synonymous. Fromond, using the word *administratio* constantly, described William as carrying out his duties "piously," "compassionately," and "humbly," with the "help of God." Acquisition of land, legal battles against the local nobility, and improvements to the cathedral, all of which Fromond described in great detail in the longest section of the work, were perfectly compatible with a bishop's personal spirituality. Though he once distinguished between doing the "Lord's work" in blessing a sick man and carrying out administrative duties in dedicating a chapel, Fromond gave little indication that he saw any contradiction between spirituality and administration.

The biographer, after William's death, was able to synthesize all aspects of the bishop's character. But the cathedral chapter seemed unable to find a successor to William who combined personal holiness with administrative ability. Faced with a choice between someone schooled in humility and someone experienced in dealing with secular affairs, the canons could not agree on the essential attributes for a worthy bishop. When William's long illness finally ended in death, the election of his successor split between a Cistercian abbot and an administrator from the secular clergy.

VI

HUGH OF NOYERS,
THE HAMMER OF THE HERETICS

Hugh of Noyers (1183-1206), like his predecessor, was described by his official biographer as very effective in temporal administration. Yet, unlike Fromond, this biographer judged his subject deficient in some areas of diocesan administration. A contemporary chronicler went further and indicated that Hugh was also deficient in piety, which kept him from being a worthy bishop.

Hugh is the first of the twelfth-century bishops of Auxerre to have, in effect, two biographers: Eustache, the cathedral canon who wrote the biography in the *Gesta pontificum Autissiodorensium,* and Robert, a canon of St.-Marien, who included many details of Hugh's pontificate in the history of the world that he wrote at the beginning of the thirteenth century. The two are contemporary accounts; Eustache wrote sometime during the pontificate of Hugh's successor, between 1207 and 1220, and Robert wrote his sections on Hugh sometime between 1207 and his own death in 1212. The two accounts are not entirely independent; phrases from one sometimes appear in the other, though the closeness of the dates makes it impossible to be sure who had read whom. Nevertheless, these two closely linked accounts give two different pictures of Hugh.

Eustache, the official biographer, admired Hugh's magnificent character, his severity towards heretics, and his care for the bishopric's temporal possessions; he was reluctant to speak harshly of his subject, but he still deplored many aspects of Hugh's administration in a biography more negative towards its subject than any other from twelfth-century Auxerre. Robert felt no need to temper his criticism. Both Eustache and Robert accused Hugh of neglect of his diocese, and Robert, as a canon of the Premonstratensian house of St.-Marien, added an indictment of Hugh's love of luxury.

Eustache's biography, the longest so far written at Auxerre (6500 words), was the first to use subheadings to separate topics. He used these subheadings quite frequently, but the smaller topics are grouped by position into several major topics. The first 400 words are a description of Hugh's family and character (including a mention of some of Hugh's deplorable habits). The next section, only 120 words long, is a description of

Hugh's defense of orthodoxy against heretics. The next section, much longer (over 700 words), concerns the bishop's improvements to episcopal manors throughout the diocese. It opens with the comment, "Although he thus was active in spiritual affairs [suppressing heresy], he was much more active in temporal affairs." This section on Hugh's care for the bishopric's temporal possessions is followed by a 750-word passage on the construction he did at his family castle, followed by an account of Hugh's defense of the bishopric's temporal possessions against laymen (a more than 300-word passage). The whole center section of the work, the longest section, thus involves Hugh's care for temporal possessions, in which Eustache included both his see's and his family's. After this long section, Eustache gave 450 words to an account of Hugh's suppression of an additional heresy and 400 words to his (unsuccessful) attempts to be translated to another diocese and his gifts to his church and cathedral chapter. The biography ends with an account of Hugh's death. Robert, writing a chronicle in which the material was arranged by years, had no similar structure; rather, he included comments on Hugh under the years in which the bishop achieved something noteworthy.

This controversial bishop was the son of the lord of Noyers, a castle located in the diocese of Langres, a short distance east of the border of the diocese of Auxerre. He was related to his predecessor, although the exact degree of their relationship is not clear; both William and Hugh were cousins of the lords of Seignelay and Pierre-Pertuis. Hugh's uncle Gui was archbishop of Sens (1176–1193), and his aunt Agnes had been abbess of St.-Julien of Auxerre (1144–c. 1174). Until 1186, the archdeacon of Auxerre was another Gui, Hugh's blood relative.[1] At the time of the death of Bishop William, Hugh had held the office of treasurer of the chapter of Auxerre for at least five years.

In spite of Hugh's well-placed ecclesiastical relatives and his own position as chapter treasurer, circumstances very similar to William's at the time of his election, Hugh's election was a long and slow process. Although William had begged the cathedral canons on his deathbed to elect his successor without delay, the see stood empty, administered by the chapter without a bishop, for nearly two years. The delay was due to an irreconcilable dispute in the chapter over the choice of a new bishop. Some of the canons elected Garmund, abbot of Pontigny, a choice which Robert of St.-Marien said was due not to Garmund's own merits but to the solicitude of his brother, highly placed in the royal curia. But not all the canons would

1. *Gallia Christiana* 12:139, no. 56.

accept Garmund, and the king, although he does not seem to have inter-fered in this election, seized the episcopal revenues when no election took place. He was exercising the royal right of *regalia*, the right to administer the temporal rights of a bishopric during a vacancy. This right had been exercised in some parts of France for several hundred years, though not at Auxerre, and Robert called the practice "illegitimate" (*contra ius*).[2]

Like more and more cathedral chapters of the late twelfth century, when faced with inability to agree on a candidate, the canons took their disputed election to Rome. But Alexander III had just died, which added to the confusion of a court where litigation was at best turbulent and im-provised; in the 1180s, papal machinery had not yet been able to catch up with the rapid growth in papal business.[3] Auxerre's election was never for-mally resolved; after over a year of fruitless delay in Rome, Garmund died, and the canons returned home to elect Hugh without any further dissent.

The Suppression of Heresy and Dissent

One of Hugh's first duties when he finally became bishop was to attend to the heresies and popular movements which had begun to grow in the region. His predecessors had not been troubled by heresy, but several different movements appeared in Auxerre in the years after 1180, when the number of heretics was increasing all over France.[4] Eustache opened and closed his description of Hugh's accomplishments as bishop with short accounts of his opposition to heretics, and he said admiringly that Hugh showed such fervor that he merited the name, "Hammer of the Heretics" (*hereticorum malleus*). Robert of St.-Marien on the other hand had a great deal of sympathy for the movements against which Hugh's enmity was turned.

The first case facing Hugh was not an actual heresy—Eustache called it a "presumption," Robert a "novelty of peace." The movement of the Capuciati had begun at Le Puy in 1183, the year Hugh became bishop of Auxerre. It was begun by a man who said that he had been commanded by the Lord in a vision to bring peace to His people. He acquired a large following of villagers and noblemen, each of whom wore a white cap and

2. Robert of St.-Marien, pp. 244–46.
3. R. W. Southern, *Western Society and the Church in the Middle Ages* (Harmonds-worth, Eng., 1970), p. 116. Geoffrey Barraclough, "The Making of a Bishop in the Middle Ages: The Part of the Pope in Law and Fact," *Catholic Historical Review* 19 (1933-34), 275-319.
4. Augustin Fliche, Christine Touzellier, and Yvonne Azais, *La Chrétienté romaine (1198-1274)*, Histoire de l'église depuis les origines jusqu'à nos jours 10 (Paris, 1950), p. 113.

a lead seal on the forehead carrying the image of the Mother of God. This group set out to destroy the strongholds of the bandits and highwaymen who had troubled the region. The movement spread rapidly northward through France and began to change within a year of its foundation. Soon the Capuciati were attacking not only bandits but all members of the nobility, including the princes who had originally helped them. Not surprisingly, the nobles and bishops soon turned on the Capuciati and crushed the movement.

Eustache called it a "very horrible and dangerous presumption." He saw no good in it, even at its beginning, but said that its fair appearance was a deceit, inspired by "an angel of Satan transforming himself into an angel of light" (cf. 2 Cor. 11.14-15). He said the movement came about when "plebeians" rebelled against their superiors, forgetting that "the wages of sin is servitude" (a curious reworking of Rom. 6.23, "the wages of sin is death"), and replacing the distinction between the great and small with "confusion." He found nothing to admire in a movement where peasants acted as the equals of princes, and he praised Hugh's quick action against the Capuciati. In Eustache's words, Hugh decided that when all political and Catholic disciplines were threatened with extermination, it was no time for "bland exhortations" but for "great undertakings." He rode out heavily armed, captured all the Capuciati in the Auxerrois, and took away their caps and lead seals. Eustache said that he then determined to make an example of them, so that no serfs (*servi*) would presume further to be insolent to lords (*domini*) (cf. 1 Peter 2.18). He imposed a large fine and forbade the wearing of hats of any kind for a year. He shortened this term, however, when Archbishop Gui of Sens, his uncle, saw peasants scorching hatless in the summer fields and moved by a "humanity" Hugh had not felt, urged the bishop to greater clemency. In this section, even though the Capuciati do not seem to have been very difficult to overcome, Eustache drew a picture of Hugh as a determined and powerful fighter, overcoming a highly dangerous threat to his authority.[5]

Robert's description of the movement was rather different. He described as highly laudable the "humility" of the Capuciati's founder and his search for peace. Like Eustache, however, Robert could not approve of the decision of the village members of the movement to turn against the entire nobility, "insolently denying subjection." He described how they were crushed, though not Hugh's part in this. Robert approved of obedience

---

5. *Gesta*, pp. 445–47.

to God and a humble desire for peace, but he did not approve of the Capuciati once they gave up their original humility to try to make themselves the equal of princes.[6]

The differences between Robert and Eustache in their attitudes toward this movement can also be seen in other contemporary chronicles. Geoffrey, the author of the *Chronicle of Limoges*, spoke very sympathetically of how the Mother of God inspired a simple carpenter to found the movement in order to bring the "serenity of peace" to the lowly. The anonymous chronicler of Laon, on the other hand, called the movement an "insane madness" (*insana rabies*), inspired not by a vision but by a desire of the people of Le Puy to bring greater income to their town if its approaches were less troubled by bandits. The story of the vision he called simple "imposture." Although he could not disapprove of the Capuciati ridding the world of bandits, he called the decision to turn next against counts and viscounts demented (*dementia*).[7] A movement such as this, that gave rise to such varied opinions, brought out the differences between Eustache and Robert, between a biographer who admired a forceful attack on any who opposed a bishop's will and a chronicler who expected humility and deference in an ecclesiastic or holy man.

In the case of the movement of the Capuciati, which was not an actual heresy, Eustache indicated that Hugh was willing to accept the villagers back in his lands once they had given up their movement and their caps. In the case of actual heresy, however, he demanded that the heretics do elaborate penance or else leave the diocese. Information on heresy in the Auxerrois comes from both Eustache's and Robert's accounts and from contemporary documents.

The chief center for heresy in the diocese was La Charité, 80 kilometers southwest of Auxerre, where Catharism flourished at the end of the twelfth century. If the heresy had already taken root before Hugh's consecration, neither he nor his predecessor noticed it, but ten years after he became bishop it had spread to the point that even the abbot of St.-Martin in nearby Nevers and the dean of Nevers cathedral were accused of Catharism and deposed at a provincial council in 1198. Hugh contacted Innocent III, who had the archbishop of Sens conduct a prolonged inquiry into the beliefs of all the citizens of La Charité in 1199. Eustache related that Hugh himself hunted down the heretics that the inquiry revealed; he allowed some to be absolved after renouncing their error and declaring their repentance on

6. Robert of St.-Marien, p. 247.
7. Geoffrey of Limoges, *Chronica Lemoviensis*, RHGF 18:219. *Chronica Laudensis*, ibid., pp. 705–06.

their knees in Auxerre cathedral, but he also "drove many away from the land of their birth" to live in Italy or among the Albigensians.[8]

Eustache clearly agreed with Hugh's position that heresies and "presumptions" must be crushed. Even if he saw a lack of "humanity" in the length of the sentence Hugh imposed on the defeated Capuciati, he had no quarrel with the defeat itself. Robert of St.-Marien, however, believed that heretics and dissenters could best be brought back to orthodoxy by persuasion, not force. Though he described how Hugh stripped stubborn heretics of their possessions or even had them burned, he only praised men who converted heretics by preaching. One such was the priest Fulk of Neuilly, from the region of Paris, a man who, inspired by God in Robert's words, preached "healthy doctrine and truth" throughout Francia, Burgundy, and Flanders, doing miracles and converting many usurers and Cathars. Robert further set up a comparison between Cistercians who had tried to overcome the Albigensian heretics with knights and footsoldiers in the generation before, gaining nothing but "fraudulent" converts who returned to their error as soon as the knights left, and those Cistercians who, as "evangelical men," went preaching on foot to convert the heretics of Toulouse. He also described with approval Bishop Humbaud, who died 100 years before he did, as a man who preached the gospel on foot, although there are no contemporary indications that Humbaud did anything of the kind. Robert clearly considered that the best way to convert heretics, the only way recommended in the Gospels, was by preaching and giving an example of holiness.[9]

Eustache's and Robert's opposing beliefs on the best way to treat heretics are found in other thinkers of the early thirteenth century; indeed an individual might change his mind about the most appropriate method. Pope Innocent III (1198–1216) originally attempted to redeem heretics from error through peaceful persuasion; he brought back to orthodoxy some semi-heretical groups such as the Waldensians. But in 1209 he changed his policy for the Cathars of southern France and sent instead of Cistercian preachers a Crusade of the French nobility. Innocent fully supported Hugh's fight against the heretics of the Auxerrois and, in 1204, also directed him to move against usurers, who he said were "worms" who

---

8. Robert of St.-Marien, pp. 245, 248. *Gesta*, p. 433. Innocent III, Letter 2.63, PL 214:602–04.

9. Robert of St.-Marien, pp. 228, 245, 258, 270. Fulk is also described by the Continuator of Otto of Freising's *Chronica*, MGH SS 20:329–31, and by Roger of Hoveden, *Chronica*, RS 51, 4:76–77. Norman Cohn makes Fulk a messianic leader of an apocalyptic cult, but the evidence does not support his judgment: *The Pursuit of the Millenium*, new ed. (New York, 1970), p. 89.

would eat holes in sacerdotal vestments, "putrid flesh" that must be cut out of a healthy body.[10]

Though Hugh thus defended orthodoxy in a manner approved by both his official biographer and the pope, Eustache indicated that he neglected more basic diocesan administration. He did not include Hugh's stand against heresy in the 250-word section at the end of the biography in which he described Hugh's administration of diocesan affairs. Rather the two passages on heresy bracket the long middle section of the work, on Hugh's care for his temporal possessions. Eustache's assessment of Hugh's diocesan *administratio* (and an indication that he did not consider the suppression of heresy part of this administration) is given at the end of his introductory passage. Hugh, he said, "would have been commended by everyone for his episcopal administration if he had showed the same fervor in spiritual affairs that he showed in temporal affairs, but he was in fact quite remiss in spiritual affairs, because of his preoccupation with temporal concerns."[11] This indictment of Hugh's diocesan administration is startlingly frank in the *Gesta's* tradition of episcopal biography. Eustache was the first of the twelfth-century biographers of Auxerre to commend his subject's temporal administration while deploring his diocesan administration.

Eustache gave very few details on Hugh's care for the needs of local houses; Robert gave none. However, the evidence provided by the charters tends to support Eustache's picture of neglect. Hugh, like all bishops of Auxerre before him, attested to gifts to local houses, but the number of such existing charters issued per year is much less than for the pontificate of William of Toucy (an average of 0.4 surviving documents per year versus 1.6), even though the total number of surviving documents from the Auxerrois increases for the late twelfth and early thirteenth centuries. In fact, the documents indicate that bishops from outside the diocese were witnesses to pious gifts or settled quarrels involving the local churches almost as often as Hugh himself, and even the count sometimes stepped in to protect the rights of local churches when Hugh did not.[12] In addition,

10. Fliche, Touzellier, and Azais, *La Chrétienté romaine*, pp. 120–25. Herbert Grundmann, *Religiöse Bewegungen im Mittelalter*, 2nd ed. (Hildesheim, 1960), pp. 135–36. Innocent III, Letter 6.321, PL 215:269–70. Jean Lebeuf, *Mémoires concernant l'histoire civile et ecclésiastique d'Auxerre*, ed. and aug. Ambroise Challe and Maximilien Quantin, 4 (Auxerre, 1855), 62, no. 89.

11. *Gesta*, p. 433: "In administratione episcopalium commendandus per omnia, si eo fervore spiritualia quo et temporalia duceret amplectanda; sed tanto erat in spiritualibus remissior quo in temporalibus ejus animus intentior habebatur."

12. Some examples of the intervention of other ecclesiastics from the first years of Hugh's pontificate: in 1185, the archbishop of Sens attested to a gift to St.-Marien

none of the new religious houses founded while Hugh was bishop were able to obtain foundation charters from him, even though the standard practice was for a bishop to give all new foundations in his diocese a charter confirming their possessions and their establishment as a corporation. Hugh's successor William of Seignelay, shortly after becoming bishop, issued foundation charters and regulations for the collegiate chapter at Toucy, the collegiate chapter of the Trinity in the crypt of Auxerre, and the Hospitallers of Montjou at Appoigny, all of which had first been established while Hugh was bishop (see below, Chapter VII).

While Hugh's charters show that he sometimes neglected the welfare of local churches, they also indicate that he was often in conflict with some of these churches, especially St.-Germain. He apparently was as determined to protect what he considered his prerogatives as to keep the diocese orthodox. The abbot of St.-Germain first complained to the pope about Hugh in 1186/7, writing Urban III that, when he came on visitations to those parish churches depending on the abbey, he demanded that his whole train be fed and housed, a train consisting of more than the 40 or 50 horses and riders allowed a bishop for such visits by Lateran III. In 1194, St.-Germain complained to Celestine III that Hugh did not render justice to the abbey when malefactors attacked it. In 1198, the abbot again wrote to the papal curia, complaining to Innocent III that Hugh had excommunicated some of the abbey's men without "manifest and rational cause," would not lift the ban unless they made a large payment of money, and refused to provide the monastery with the chrism and holy oil or to administer the rites of consecration of altars, benediction of new abbots, or ordination of monks promoted in orders. The popes instructed St.-Germain not to house more horses and men than the maximum specified by Lateran III and to seek out another bishop for justice and sacraments if there were such a "defect" in their own. Here the pope, like Eustache, found Hugh remiss in diocesan affairs.[13]

Hugh's quarrels with the nuns of St.-Julien were even more heated. The abbess of St.-Julien claimed rights to collect dead branches, receive the fee of mainmort, and present priests in parish churches in and around the

---

from Stephen of Pierre-Pertuis (Quantin 2.345, pp. 358–59); in 1186, the bishop of Autun attested to a pious gift to Reigny (ibid., 2.360, pp. 370–71); in 1188, the archbishop attested to a pious gift to Pontigny (ibid., 2.384, pp. 392–93). Bishop Hugh is mentioned in none of these charters. See also Quantin 3.27, pp. 12–13 (1203), in which the count rather than the bishop acted to protect St.-Marien from the noisy presence of townspeople on the house's land.

13. Hefele-Leclercq, *Histoire des conciles*, 5, 2:1091. Quantin 2.366, 451, pp. 376, 462–63. Innocent III, Letters 1.181, 184, PL 214:163–64.

episcopal city of Gy-l'Evêque; in addition she claimed Hugh owed her a small annual rent of money and grain for a house and some land in Auxerre. Hugh denied all this, and the case was appealed to the pope, who in 1196 designated the bishops of Nevers and Sens as arbiters. In 1197, they decided the case entirely in favor of the nuns, but Hugh would not agree for another year, until the archbishop of Sens received a mandate from the pope to force Hugh to yield. Even in areas of apparently minimal significance, Hugh seems to have been determined to struggle at length to retain his rights and prerogatives. Like many ecclesiastics of the end of the twelfth century, Hugh preferred to spend time and money on apparently trivial cases rather than have a papal decision give permanence to his loss of a "lawful right."[14]

Hugh's determined defense of his rights also led him into several quarrels with his chapter. Hugh was the first bishop of Auxerre known to have quarreled with his chapter since the nepotism scandal under Hugh of Mâcon fifty years earlier. The chapter, under its elected head, Dean William, was gaining a certain belligerent autonomy, a development fairly common at the beginning of the thirteenth century.[15] Eustache preferred to pass over these quarrels in silence, but details are provided by contemporary documents and by the biographer of Dean William, who succeeded Hugh as bishop.

The first known quarrel between bishop and chapter took place when Dean William declared that he, rather than the bishop, should judge all ecclesiastical cases arising within Auxerre. Hugh disagreed, and the quarrel became sharpest when Auxerre was placed under interdict (for the excesses of the count of Auxerre, as will be discussed below). William suspended some priests who did not observe the interdict. The priests complained to the bishop, and Hugh reinstated them. William appealed to the archbishop, who decided that the priests should make satisfaction to the dean for their disobedience before resuming their offices. On another occasion, Hugh, building a new episcopal palace at Regennes, cut some trees in a nearby forest that belonged to the chapter. Led again by Dean William, the chapter objected to this "injury," and Hugh was obliged to transport the logs to the gates of the cathedral in his own carts.[16]

14. *Gallia Christiana* 12:142–43, no. 60. Quantin 2.471, pp. 479–80. Arch. Yonne H 1741. Southern, *Western Society and the Church*, p. 116.
15. Jean-François Lemarignier, Jean Gaudemet, and Guillaume Mollat, *Institutions ecclésiastiques*, Histoire des institutions françaises au moyen âge 3 (Paris, 1962), pp. 191–92.
16. *Gesta*, pp. 454–55.

A third quarrel between Hugh and a member of his chapter began in 1202 when, for a reason that is obscure, Hugh excommunicated the archpriest of Auxerre. The archpriest had become an important figure in the diocese in the late twelfth century; he held authority over all the priests of the city and served as the bishop's chief assistant in liturgical functions. The archpriest appealed to the archbishop of Sens, who absolved him when Hugh refused. Hugh complained to Innocent III that his rights had been violated; the pope agreed, saying that the archpriest, separated from the church by excommunication, should not have been able to appeal to the archbishop. Hugh, who frequently used the weapon of excommunication, was doubtless pleased to hear the pope's decision that it would lead to contempt for ecclesiastical sentencing if excommunicates were able to appeal without the permission of the excommunicating bishop.[17]

The biographer of Dean William had no sympathy for Hugh and described these quarrels as triumphs for William against usurpations of rights. Eustache, however, attempted to show that Hugh's relations with his chapter were amicable, giving a list of all the bishop's gifts to the canons (a very brief list, compared to the gifts of some of his predecessors). He said that Hugh gave the canons the church of Oisy, to help pay for their daily bread, and also gave them 100 solidi from the church of St.-Bris to establish his anniversary. (Fromond stated earlier that William of Toucy gave the chapter the latter gift to establish his own anniversary; either one of the biographers was mistaken about the source of the 100 solidi the canons received, or else Hugh doubled the chapter's income from St.-Bris.)[18] Eustache, not even mentioning the quarrels between Hugh and his chapter, indicated by his listing of the bishop's gifts to the canons that Hugh was concerned for their temporal welfare as well as his own.

It is understandable that Eustache apparently preferred to pass over Hugh's quarrels with the churches of Auxerre with no more than the simple comment that he neglected the welfare of local houses and a short list of his gifts to his chapter. An account of a contentious bishop would hardly have been an edifying addition to the collected biographies. Eustache did, however, admit to Hugh's neglect. He indicated that the bishop, in preserving his own interests, neglected his pastoral duties toward the local people. According to Eustache, when Hugh fortified his family castle of Noyers, he forbade the local villagers to come up the hill to use

17. Innocent III, Letter 5.157, PL 214:1171-72. For the office of archpriest, see Gabriel LeBras, *Institutions ecclésiastiques de la Chrétienté médiévale*, Histoire de l'église depuis les origines jusqu'à nos jours 12 (Paris, 1959-64), p. 481.
18. *Gesta*, pp. 429-30, 448.

the castle church as they always had, for fear they might be disguised enemies or spies.[19]

Episcopal Magnificence

Though Hugh was unmindful of the requirements of good diocesan administration, according to his biographer and his charters, he involved himself fully in the demands of temporal administration. He improved episcopal property throughout the diocese and defended it from the count in a manner that both his biographers called "magnificent."

Eustache found this magnificence entirely appropriate in a bishop. At the beginning of the biography, where earlier biographers had generally given brief descriptions of their subjects' piety and virtues, Eustache described Hugh as if he were a powerful secular lord; Hugh, he said, was outstanding because of the excellence of his blood but even more outstanding for his "magnificence of spirit." Eustache made it clear that his magnificence was no means a religious quality. "For, as is the habit of noblemen, he acted in many things with secular magnificence, and . . . with a multiplication of journeys, a numerous train of clerics and knights, a large attendance of domestic servants, and a magnificent equipage, he matched the fame of his ancestors."[20] Eustache also described Hugh's love for the company of knights; the bishop, he said, often discussed military tactics with them, feeling "such affection" for them that, when they were at home, he acted as only one among them, though when they went out he was careful to preserve his prerogatives. There was clearly no place for humility in the character of such a bishop, and Eustache never described Hugh as humble, though this formulaic description had been used by the earlier twelfth-century biographers (even if reinterpreted, as by the biographer of William of Toucy). Eustache and Hugh's own charters sometimes used the term "the humble" as a synonym for clerics, but the term described their legal status, not their virtues or economic condition; poor laymen were also never included among the humble. In fact, clerics were more often described by such terms as "the knights of the Church Triumphant" than by terms of humility. Eustache in fact generally described humility not as a virtue but a punishment. Hugh was proud, he said, to teach his opponents "humility under the powerful hand of God,"[21] a provocative reworking of

19. Ibid., p. 438.

20. Ibid., pp. 431–32: "Nam, more nobilium, in multa degebat magnificentia seculari; et . . . in evectionum multiplicitate, numeroso clericorum et militum comitatu, multa domesticorum frequentia et apparatu magnifico, majorum suorum titulos adequabat."

21. Ibid., p. 442: ". . . non deficiebat, donec illis humilitatis sub potenti manu Dei ad honorem ejus et sponse sue ecclesie finem atingeret commendandum."

1 Peter 5.6, in which the elders of the church are urged to humble themselves under the powerful hand of God. Eustache said that Hugh had "never learned to live a withdrawn life,"[22] and he saw no reason why he should.

Eustache was not the only biographer of the early thirteenth century to describe a bishop's power and display with approval. The biographer of Englebert of Cologne (1216–1225) said, "as I may remember to his praise," that the bishop had more glory, wealth, and power than any of his predecessors. This biographer only used the term "humility" when giving a long formulaic list of his subject's many virtues. Like Eustache, this biographer's concept of proper episcopal behavior did not require adoption of a monastic style of life.[23] But while Eustache found secular magnificence and knightly companions admirable in themselves, he felt they could lead to actions extremely undesirable in a bishop. Thus, though he admired the equipage and display which were the "habit of noblemen," Eustache said that Hugh also had the "desire for having which is characteristic of the powerful." Under the heading, "In what areas his character could be reproved" (*In quo mores ejus poterant argui*), he said that this "desire for having" led to "exactions, oppressions, and usurpations of rights not his own, and, when he was angry, to a lax rein on his desires to injure and ruin."[24] The biographer of Englebert of Cologne had made no similar comment that personal magnificence in a bishop could lead to oppression.

Though Eustache strongly disapproved of Hugh's "oppression," he could not but admire his magnificence; he never compared it to the sin of pride. Robert of St.-Marien on the other hand did not view this episcopal characteristic with approval. He criticized Hugh, as Eustache had not, for a love of "heavy spending" and of "knightly deeds," as well as for his "lack of clemency" and "immoderate exactions."[25] Robert would have greatly preferred a bishop who conformed to the model of a monk or a canon regular, as is clear from a comparison of the ecclesiastics he considered

---

22. Ibid., pp. 431–32: ". . . et vitam agere privatam indocilis. . . ."
23. Englebert in fact was considered a saint after his death, though this sainthood was largely due to his having been "martyred" by the local count: Caesar of Heisterbach, *Vita, Passio, et Miracula S. Engelberti*, AASS Nov. 3:644–81.
24. *Gesta*, pp. 432–33: "Omnibus favorabilis, nisi habendi cupiditas que omne pene potentes exagitat ad exactiones et oppressiones subditorum et usurpanda jura non sua . . . et nisi, contra quemlibet indignatione concepto, ruine et nocendi libidini immoderate plerumque frena laxaret."
25. Robert of St.-Marien, p. 270: "Nam in sibi subditos minus clemens exstitit eosque inmodicis exactionibus aggravavit. Erat quippe in expensis profusior, amans conturbia militum et militarium actuum solitus pompam plus prosequi quam sacerdotali competeret gravitari."

praiseworthy and those with whom he found fault. His highest praise was reserved for Milo, abbot of St.-Marien, who lived very simply, retired from the world, practicing frugality. He condemned William, archbishop of Reims, for his prodigality in spending, and Rotrou, bishop of Châlons, for his luxury and secular activities. The spending which Eustache took as a sign of magnificence, a Ciceronian if not a Christian virtue, Robert took as an indication of the vice of luxury.[26] Robert, a Premonstratensian canon, considered that all ecclesiastics should live humbly, but the cathedral canons of Auxerre no longer took this view.

The magnificence which both of Hugh's biographers noted is especially evident in Hugh's ambitious building program. Eustache detailed with admiration the improvements Hugh made to episcopal *villae*; Robert mentioned these *villae* only in passing and without Eustache's open approval. Eustache described how Hugh added a new wine cellar and a new kitchen to the episcopal palace at Auxerre. Without mentioning the quarrel over logs with the chapter, he described the palace of "magnificent" nobility and beauty he built at Regennes, just outside Appoigny, to replace the old house, which was "humble in form and material" and thus unfit to be the house of a bishop. As the palace of Regennes lay on the bank of the Yonne in a shallow loop of the river, Hugh tried to make the site impregnable by digging a ditch to put Regennes on an island; he was adding a massive wall when the count of Champagne persuaded him to stop. Eustache went on to describe Hugh's other improvements to episcopal *villae*. He created a delightful residence he called Beaurepaire at Charbuy by turning thickets into gardens and swamps into fishponds; he built episcopal houses of "immense nobility" at Toucy and Cosne; and he heavily fortified the episcopal house at Varzy. Other bishops of Auxerre had constructed buildings on episcopal property, but none had done as much as Hugh. He built magnificent residences strong enough so that a bishop would never feel in danger, residences Eustache considered entirely appropriate for a bishop.[27]

Immediately following his description of Hugh's improvements to episcopal property, Eustache recorded his improvements to his family castle. Eustache made very little distinction between these two types of temporal activities, introducing the section on Hugh's family property with the comment, "I shall now introduce into this work a discussion of what he did in the noble castle of Noyers which he inherited." When Hugh's brother Clarembaud, lord of Noyers, died on crusade in 1190, leaving his only son a young boy, Hugh took up the administration of the

26. Ibid., pp. 262–65.
27. *Gesta*, pp. 433–36, 439–40. Robert of St.-Marien, p. 270.

castellany; his nephew Milo had no share in the government of his patrimony until after Hugh's death. Robert of St.-Marien did not mention Noyers at all, but Eustache gave many details on how Hugh made his castle, already well defended by its natural position at the top of a hill in the loop of a river, practically impregnable. He built strong new walls, made preparations to have food and water brought into the castle in baskets and pipes, and made everyone pass a rigorous security check before entering the castle.[28]

Only after an enthusiastic description of the fortifications at Noyers, which he said impressed even the duke of Burgundy, did Eustache comment, "It was a magnificent work, and it would have been worthy of great admiration and commendation if he had not there converted the possessions of the men under his care into wood and stone and consumed the greater part of the episcopal goods, which could better have been applied to the requirements of the church or the needs of the poor."[29] Though Eustache considered the fortification of a "magnificent" castle a suitable activity for a bishop, he objected to the use of ecclesiastical funds for other than ecclesiastical purposes. Once again, Hugh had neglected his pastoral duties.

Hugh's care for his temporal possessions was not entirely restricted to castles and episcopal palaces. Eustache also recorded with approval that he made a number of improvements in the cathedral: he widened several windows to let in more light, took out two altars on the side to make the nave wider, broke out new doors, repaved the floor, and decorated the walls and ceilings with paintings. For the cathedral's decoration, he gave several immense hangings and covered the old cross with silver, for which expense he was still in debt at his death. While spending great amounts of money on these projects, Hugh also increased episcopal revenues, with the result that, according to Eustache, at the time of his death he left scarcely any debts beyonu the payment for the silver-casing of the old cross.[30] However, William of Toucy had left no debts at all, in spite of the money he spent buying property.

Eustache gave a few details on how the bishop increased his revenues. At the end of the twelfth century, many secular and ecclesiastical lords

28. Ernest Petit, *Histoire des ducs de Bourgogne de la race capétienne*, 3 (Paris, 1889), 366-67, no. 852. *Gesta*, pp. 436-38.

29. *Gesta*, p. 438: ". . . magnifica quidem opera et multa admiratione digna et commendatione, nisi ibi hominium sue commissiorum custodie substantias in ligna convertisset et lapides, et bona pro magna parte consumpsisset episcopalia, que melius fuerant aut ecclesie utilitatibus aut pauperum necessitatibus aplicanda."

30. Ibid., pp. 448-49.

made close accounting of their income, with a view to how it might be increased. Since technological improvements had increased the yield of such sought-after crops as wine-grapes, attention was often turned to obtaining a share of these crops. In keeping with this trend, Hugh made an agreement with his men at Varzy that he would free them of such customary dues as mainmort, the "March taille" of 5 solidi from every household paid in March, and the fees called "haymaking" and "raking" due in the fall. (These were labor dues that had been converted to a monetary payment sometime in the early twelfth century.) The men at Varzy in turn agreed to pay the wine tithe fully, under the supervision of the bishop's men; they had previously paid only a fraction of this tithe. It was natural that Hugh should have preferred a tenth of the grape harvest to a fixed income from sources such as the "March taille," which may have been a sizeable payment a century earlier but had been greatly eroded by the inflation of the twelfth century. According to Eustache, once Hugh began collecting the wine tithe instead of customary dues, which had been considered demeaning by the men of Varzy, his annual income from these lands increased from less than 100 to 500 or 600 pounds a year.[31]

Eustache considered that Hugh's defense of his rights and property, his improvements to episcopal *villae*, and his efforts to increase his revenues all made him an excellent temporal administrator. His emphasis on such episcopal duties was not unique in a time when episcopal administration was becoming increasingly complex and legalistic, demanding a great deal of a bishop's attention. Even such a bishop as Hugh of Lincoln (1186–1200), a Carthusian who, unlike Hugh, was canonized by the pope within 20 years of his death and was constantly called "humble" by his biographer, was remembered with praise by his biographer for having carried out his duties "forcefully" (*strenue*), even excommunicating a royal official who was "violent and rapacious" toward his church.[32] Though Eustache said that Hugh of Noyers gave little attention to the "spiritual" affairs of the diocese, and Robert of St.-Marien complained pointedly about bishops who were "raised to ecclesiastical honors and then neglected those honors" in favor of an "effusion of goods, pomp, and glory," neither one considered that Hugh neglected the temporal rights, property, and income adhering to the bishopric.

---

31. Ibid., p. 440. *Gallia Christiana* 12:146, no. 62. Georges Duby, *Guerriers et paysans, VII–XIIe siècle: Premier essor de l'économie européenne* (Paris, 1973), pp. 252, 297–99.
32. Alexander of Canterbury, *Vita Sancti Hugonis episcopi Lincolniensis*, PL 153: 937–1114.

They also agreed that Hugh put up a splendid defense against the attacks of the count of Auxerre. When Hugh became bishop in 1183, the three counties of Auxerre, Nevers, and Tonnerre were ruled by the countess Mathilda, widow of Gui. Gui's only son, William, had just died while still a boy. At the time of Count Gui's death in 1176, Louis VII had taken his two children, William and Agnes, under royal protection. In 1184, less than two years after her brother's death, Philip II gave Agnes in marriage to his cousin Peter of Courtenay, to whom he also gave the counties of Nevers and Auxerre—Mathilda kept Tonnerre until 1192, when she retired to Fontevrault. Agnes and Peter had one daughter, named Mathilda for her grandmother, who inherited all three counties when her mother died in 1193. In 1199, King Philip married Mathilda to Hervé, lord of Donzy. Hervé thus became count of Nevers, but Peter of Courtenay retained the counties of Auxerre and Tonnerre. A glance at the genealogy chart (Figure 3) will show that Peter's marriage to Agnes was within the seven forbidden degrees, but no one at the time seemed to consider it incestuous, and the couple apparently did not need papal dispensation to marry. Hervé and Mathilda, however, needed a special papal dispensation to remain married, as his paternal grandmother and her maternal grandmother's father were sister and brother (both were the children of Duke Hugh II of Burgundy).[33]

Both Peter and Hervé, but especially Peter, were formidable opponents for the bishop of Auxerre. Eustache described them as evil men whom only a bishop as vigorous as Hugh could hope to control. He described Peter as "unrestrained" in his character, a man of "terrible wrath" who could not be held back from doing injury. His person and his lands were put under interdict repeatedly; Eustache said that the divine service would scarcely have been celebrated at all in Auxerre while he was count if the bishop and his chapter had not decided to lift the ban at the cathedral whenever he was out of Auxerre and then to reimpose silence when he returned. The interdict was partially lifted this way at the cathedral, and by papal privilege at St.-German, because, according to Eustache, it was feared that heresy would grow if the churches stood silent.[34]

Hugh's determination to keep Auxerre under interdict while the unrepentant count was in the city led to his sharpest quarrel with Peter, in

33. Robert of St.-Marien, pp. 244, 259. *Gesta*, pp. 440–41. Quantin 2.330, p. 347. Petit, *Ducs de Bourgogne*, 3:318–19, no. 876. For the difficulties caused by the broad definition of "consanguinuity" at the end of the twelfth century and the relative ease with which dispensations could be acquired, see John W. Baldwin, *Masters, Princes, and Merchants: The Social Views of Peter the Chanter and His Circle*, 1 (Princeton, 1970), 332–34.

34. *Gesta*, p. 441. Innocent III, Letter 6.23, PL 215:27–28.

1203/4. Eustache and Robert of St.-Marien gave very similar accounts of this quarrel, which they both presented as a demonstration of the strong episcopal stand necessary against secular depravity.[35] Peter, newly absolved from his most recent excommunication, plundered a church and blinded one of the bishop's vassals. Hugh, weathering "formidable storms" to uphold ecclesiastical rights "like an insurmountable wall," in Eustache's words, immediately renewed the excommunication and the interdict. While the count stayed in Auxerre, no church services, including burials, could be held. A woman whose boy had died and could not be buried made an unfortunate attempt to complain to the count, which only aroused his famous rage. Taking the body, Peter hurried to the episcopal palace, dug up the floor of the bishop's bedroom, and buried the boy there. Not satisfied, he then ordered Hugh out of the city and all the clerics of Auxerre with him. Hugh fled to Pontigny, but Peter drove him from there entirely out of the diocese.

From self-styled exile, Hugh wrote to Innocent III and received a letter of consolation and support. The pope commanded Peter to make satisfaction to the bishop for the salvation of his soul, urged the king to remember it was his duty to help the church and thus to assist Hugh, and reprimanded the archbishop of Sens for not having forced Peter to make restitution.[36] Pressured by the pope, the archbishop of Sens, and his own uncle, the bishop of Bourges, Peter finally recalled Hugh from exile and did public penance. Both Eustache and Robert described in detail how, before all the people and clergy of Auxerre, Peter dug up the boy's body, which had now lain for months in the episcopal palace, and, walking barefoot, carried it to the cemetery for burial. Eustache considered him to have been humiliated by God, "who bends the necks of kings" (perhaps a reference to Josh. 10.24).

According to both accounts, Peter gave Hugh no more trouble. Thus, both Robert and Eustache described the bishop as very successful in maintaining episcopal rights against this particularly vicious opponent. Eustache went on to describe how Hugh, with his firm care for the temporal possessions of his office, also took action against some of the count's men. He related how Hugh captured one Peter of Corcio, who had appropriated ecclesiastical land after already incurring Hugh's enmity by buying some property the bishop had wanted for himself. Hugh punished this captured knight by making a public spectacle of him, having him driven around Auxerre in a cart pulled by deformed horses. This revenge, according to

---

35. *Gesta*, pp. 442–43. Robert of St.-Marien, p. 267.
36. Innocent III, Letters 6.149–52, PL 215:160–68.

Eustache, showed that God "deposes the powerful from their seat and exalts the humble," though this revenge scarcely seems to have been the act of a humble man. When another of the count's knights, Eraud of Châteauneuf, murdered someone in the church of Notre-Dame-la-Dehors, Hugh brought charges of heresy against him at a legatine council held in Paris in 1202. Eraud was convicted of the "bulgarian" heresy and released to the secular arm to be burned. Evidently Hugh used every means at his disposal to fight against the local nobility.[37]

Though Eustache emphasized the hostility between Hugh and the local nobility to highlight Hugh's successes, some of Hugh's charters show that on occasion he cooperated with the count on projects in which they both had an interest. In 1193, Hugh and the heads of other local churches agreed to contribute to Count Peter's construction of new city walls, though Hugh stipulated that this contribution could not set a precedent. Walls to encircle the town that had grown up around the old Roman city had been begun sometime in the middle of the twelfth century, and Peter was now finishing the last section along the river. In 1194, Peter asked Hugh to be a guarantor, along with the bishops of Sens, Langres, Autun, and Nevers, of his agreement with the townspeople of Auxerre, in which he freed them from some payments and obligations and detailed their obligations in such other areas as army service and justice. Hugh's permission may have been necessary if this agreement was considered an "innovation" in the city, but the presence of Hugh and the other bishops was also a guarantee to both the count and the townspeople that the agreement would be kept.[38]

Hugh, who did not hestiate to defend his rights against the most powerful lords of the region, also did not hesitate when facing the king, according to both his charters and his admiring biographer. When Hervé of Donzy married the heiress of Nevers in 1199 and granted the king his city of Gien in return for the county of Nevers, Hugh did not let the king forget that Hervé had held the city of Gien in fief from the bishop; William of Toucy had extracted a deathbed homage for it from the previous lord of Donzy. Hugh made the king agree to continue to pay the annual 100 pounds of wax that Hervé had paid, and, in return for letting the fief be transferred without requiring liege homage from the king, Hugh obtained an end to the royal right of *gîte* in the entire diocese.[39]

37. *Gesta*, pp. 439, 443–45. Robert of St.-Marien, p. 260. Hefele–Leclercq, *Histoire des conciles*, 5, 2:1229. Mansi 22:439–40.
38. Quantin 2.443, 450, pp. 449, 459–62.
39. Quantin 3.36, p. 18. *Gesta*, pp. 438–39.

Hugh's forceful defense of his rights and his concern for his church's temporal possessions and his own certainly made him an effective administrator in at least some of the duties Eustache and Robert saw as appropriate in a bishop. Though Hugh, with his heavily fortified *villae* and castle, seems in many respects like a man who would have made a better secular lord than an ecclesiastical lord, he was considered by his contemporaries to be a very effective bishop. Because of what Eustache called his "industry and prudence" in secular affairs, the canons of Langres asked Hugh to protect their possessions while their disputed election was resolved, and at least some if not all of the canons of Sens chose him as their new archbishop when that see fell vacant in 1199. Hugh's aspirations to be archbishop, however, were frustrated by Innocent III, who refused to allow the translation, preferring his old master Peter of Corbeil for the position. Innocent wrote the canons that their selection of Hugh was "unworthy" (*indignus*), not because of the method of election, but because of the person elected. According to Innocent's letters and the *Gesta Innocentii*, his rejection of Hugh was based largely on the fact that Hugh had not observed the interdict laid on France that same year, when King Philip II had refused to take back his wife, Ingeborg of Denmark. Hugh was the only French bishop to refuse to promulgate the interdict, saying loftily that the king had no lands in the diocese, as the bishop held them all directly from God (contrast Alain, p. 76). Hugh may have been reluctant to observe the general interdict in part because his diocese was enjoying one of the brief interludes when it was not already under interdict due to the excesses of the count of Auxerre. But Innocent labeled Hugh's excuses "frivolous"; for him, Hugh had not carried out the proper duties of a bishop.[40]

Conclusions

Eustache, Robert of St.-Marien, and Innocent III all regarded Hugh as very effective in certain areas of temporal administration, especially defense of episcopal rights against the count, but they also all found something to reprove in his conduct. Eustache said that the bishop oppressed those under him and misappropriated episcopal funds, Robert that he succumbed to the sin of pride. Innocent rebuked him for not readily obeying each papal order. Each of them expected something different in an ideal bishop, and each was disappointed in some respects by Hugh.

40. *Gesta*, pp. 444–48. Robert of St.-Marien, pp. 259–60. *Gesta Innocentii papae III*, PL 214:xcviii–xcix, cii–ciii. Innocent III, Letter 3.20, PL 214:898–99. Hefele-Leclercq, *Histoire des conciles*, 5, 2:1227.

By all accounts Hugh was an awe-inspiring person who affected the lives of all around him, in death as in life. Unlike William of Toucy, who lingered toward death amid singing, prayers, and lamentations, Hugh died quite suddenly at Rome, where he had gone "both for a pilgrimage and to advance some business," and his death was signalled, both at Rome and at Auxerre, by a series of horrifying signs. According to Eustache's account, in Rome, three days before his unanticipated death, there were strange rumbles in the night as of a building collapsing, while at the same time near Auxerre the house Hugh had built at Appoigny and the municipal walls he had erected at Varzy both fell in. On the day of the bishop's death in Rome, a cathedral canon at Auxerre saw the bishop coming toward him in a horrifying (*horrenda*) vision that came not in a dream but in broad daylight. The bishop told the stupefied canon, "Come, follow, for I go before"; he was calling the canon to follow him into the grave, for the man fell ill immediately and died three days later. Before Hugh's companions in Rome could return to Auxerre with the news, Eustache saw one of them in a dream, his face altered by sorrow, saying, "Death is near, pestilence prompt, health distant." Eustache finished this remarkable description by asking his readers to pray that this "magnificent" man might find a place among the saints and the elect. He gave no indication that Hugh had already done so.[41]

Eustache did not describe anything in Hugh comparable to the piety and spiritual orientation that earlier biographers had seen in their bishops. This is evident especially in his treatment of humility. From the evidence of the biblical quotations that he used, Eustache considered humility a punishment to be visited on the haughty, the sinful, and the bishop's enemies, rather than an appropriate episcopal virtue. He made servitude rather than death the wages of sin. He had Hugh teach the powerful humility under the powerful hand of God rather than learn humility himself. He insisted that servants should obey their masters and that God bends the necks of kings before churchmen. Hugh was one of the powerful who should be retained in his position of authority over the lowly; any belief that all men should be equal represented an angel of Satan disguised as an angel of light. Not only should the lowly be kept in an inferior position, but those more powerful than Hugh, such as his secular opponents, should be cast down. Robert of St.-Marien on the other hand found humility necessary in any ecclesiastic, including a bishop, and deplored its lack in Hugh.

41. *Gesta*, pp. 449–50.

No such conflicts over a bishop's proper role are evident in the biography of Hugh's successor. William of Seignelay was no less ready to defend ecclesiastical rights, but his biographer was able to describe him without the reservations that Eustache and Robert felt about Hugh. The biographer found in his subject a man with spiritual qualities and a concern for diocesan administration, not merely ability in temporal administration.

VII

WILLIAM OF SEIGNELAY
AND EPISCOPAL ADMINISTRATION

William of Seignelay (bishop of Auxerre 1207–1220, bishop of Paris 1220–1223) is a suitable figure with which to conclude this study. He appears to have been particularly successful at balancing the competing demands of the episcopal office. He was described in his biography as effectively combining personal sanctity, concern for local religious houses, and vigorous defense of episcopal property against those whom the biographer called evil men, meaning above all the counts. He left a longer biography and more documents than any other twelfth-century bishop of Auxerre, and thus his episcopate yields a great deal of information on the problems and choices that many bishops had to face at the beginning of the thirteenth century. His anonymous biographer described him, in a biography that has some hagiographical elements, as a kind and benevolent man; a number of William's documents, however, reveal that in some cases William was as unyielding toward local ecclesiastics as Hugh of Noyers had been.

The biography begins with a description of William's family. Over 400 words are devoted to the sanctity of his relatives, among them his mother, whose death was attended by miracles, and St. Bernard, his cousin once removed. This section is followed by an equally long passage on William's boyhood and how he became a cleric, a 550-word passage on his activities as dean of Auxerre, and a 300-word description of William's love for his brother Manasses. Then at last the biographer turned to William's election. In 500 words he described how William was elected to Auxerre after refusing two other sees, and in 350 words how he obtained the regalia of Auxerre from the king upon his election. The events leading up to the bishop's assumption of office, which earlier biographers covered in a few sentences, are here treated in a section that is longer than the whole of many of the earlier biographies. The next section, a 500-word passage on William's character and virtues, marks a return to the pattern typical of these biographies, but it is followed by nearly 1400 words on the deeds of William's brother Manasses as bishop of Orléans. Only then did the biographer begin his account of William's achievements as bishop of Auxerre: "Let us now return to William, whose history we set out to write."

The long section detailing William's episcopal activities is divided into three unequal parts. The first, a 1000-word passage beginning with the comment, "William actively and effectively set out to make improvements to the churches when he took up his duties," is devoted to liturgical innovations, renovations of the episcopal palace, and the establishment of several houses of canons and nuns in the diocese. Next, in a 400-word passage under the headings "What he acquired" and "Concerning fiefs," the biographer described how William obtained liege homage from several powerful laymen of the region. The last section is the longest—over 1500 words on William's construction of a new cathedral, attended by numerous miracles. The final 2200 words of the biography are a description of William's translation to Paris, with concluding sentences on the conditions in which he left his see, a short passage on his achievements in his new see, and an account of his "blessed" death.

Since William's family is emphasized in this biography more than the families of any of his predecessors had been, it is likely that the biographer was a relative of William's, although it is impossible to identify him any more closely. William was son of Bochard, brother of the powerful lord of Seignelay. Another brother of Bochard was Gui, archbishop of Sens (1176–1193). Since Hugh of Noyers had also been a nephew of Archbishop Gui, Hugh and William must have been cousins, but the biographer did not mention this relationship. He described instead how William and his older brother Manasses learned their letters at the cathedral school of Sens under their uncle, who made them respectively treasurer and archdeacon of Sens cathedral. From these posts, William was promoted to dean of Auxerre and then bishop, and Manasses was elected bishop of Orléans. Though the biographer did not mention him, the obituary of Auxerre indicates that another of William's relatives, his nephew Andrew, became archdeacon of Auxerre while William was bishop there.[1]

William's biographer indicated that his election to Auxerre was the third opportunity he had had to become a bishop. The biographer—giving a version somewhat different from those of Eustache and the biographer of Innocent III—said that when the see of Sens fell vacant in 1199, a great many of the canons wanted either William or his brother Manasses as their next archbishop. Only when each said that he was unworthy and suggested instead Hugh of Noyers did the chapter of Sens elect Hugh, an election that was overturned by Innocent III (see above, p. 117). A few years later,

---

1. *Gesta*, p. 453. Auguste Longnon, Alexandre Vidier, and Léon Mirot, eds., *Obituaires de la province de Sens*, 3, *Diocèses d'Orléans, d'Auxerre, et de Nevers* (Paris, 1909), p. 261. For William's family, see Constance B. Bouchard, "The Structure of a Twelfth-Century French Family: The Lords of Seignelay," *Viator* 10 (1979), 39–56.

according to William's biographer, he was chosen as bishop by the chapter of Nevers, but William would not accept the office, saying that he preferred to live a quiet life in the company of his brother. His biographer reported that he regretted this decision once he became bishop of Auxerre, for Nevers was a poorer church than the see he now headed.[2] William's unwillingness to be elected, according to his biographer, went far beyond any standard protestations of unworthiness and came from a genuine modesty. He did not use the term *humilitas*, but he expressed a similar concept in saying that William was not ambitious (*procul erat ambitio*) and that he was ashamed to be found at the head of a wealthy see.

William at first resisted his election to the see of Auxerre as vigorously as he had resisted election to Sens and Nevers. The biographer, considering his reluctance to be a demonstration of virtue, gave full details. The canons, he said, agreed *per compromissionem* on William after an initial decision that either William or his brother Manasses would make an excellent bishop. William, however, insisted that Manasses, older than he, should be bishop; the insistence of each that the other should take the office led, according to the biographer, to the first discord that had ever risen between them. But William's resistance was finally broken down by the archbishop of Sens, and Manasses was elected bishop of Orléans within the year.[3]

Sanctity of Family and Office

The starting point for the biographer's discussion of William's virtuous nature was the sanctity of his relatives. William, said the biographer, had inherited "firmness of character" from his father and "holiness of life" from his mother.[4] His mother Aanor was a daughter of the lord of Montbard and a cousin of St. Bernard (whose mother was the sister of the lord of Montbard). This relationship to Bernard is only the first-mentioned of many connections with the Cistercian Order that recur throughout William's biography, although there is no indication that William had any inclination to adopt a life of Cistercian poverty himself.[5] The biographer presented Bernard and William's mother as models of holiness with which to compare the bishop. Bernard, he said, had been placed in the catalogue

---

2. *Gesta*, pp. 458-59: ". . . cum maxima penitudine et cordis amaritudine remorare solebat, pungente eum conscientia quod Autissiodorensem velut ditiorem Niveronsi tanquam pauperi ecclesie pretulisset."

3. Ibid., p. 459.

4. Ibid., p. 451: ". . . claram ab utroque parente duxit originem, ex parte patris insuperabilis constantie, ex parte matris vite sanctioris existens."

5. Chevalier is mistaken in making William himself a Cistercian: *Bio-Bibliographie* 1:1980.

of saints because of the "merit of his life" and the "many miracles" he did, both before and after his death. The life of William's mother was also noteworthy for its merits and its miracles. The biography put special emphasis on her adoption of poverty, explicitly called *humilitas*. She made herself "lowly in both her person and her possessions," he said, as befitted a "handmaiden of Christ," and ministered to the poor, as befitted one of "Christ's poor." The servile words *servilis* and *ancilla*, which had not been used to characterize peasants for the last century, were here used to describe spiritual humility. The biographer also remarked that Aanor was "assiduous" in her prayers, "frequently in church," and "alert" during the divine office, essentially equating holiness with observance of liturgical forms.[6]

This virtuous woman's death was accompanied by a miracle which the biographer included to indicate that the holy attributes he had just described were outward signs of her blessedness. Dying at the family castle of Esnon, she asked for her body to be carried to Pontigny, thirteen kilometers away, where her husband was already buried. The cortege arrive there through a terrible storm, yet the funeral candles that had been lit around her were still burning peacefully. William's biographer apologized for digressing to tell this story, saying that God had made this woman an example of "humility" and "goodness" and that the miracle came about for the "glory of God" and "man's instruction." The digression is an example of the sort of undoubted sanctity with which William's biographer would compare the bishop's spiritual life.[7]

The biographer said that William followed his mother in his love of the divine service and his personal goodness, but he did not draw a direct comparison between Aanor's humility and William's sense of unworthiness for the episcopal office. In fact, he did not use the term *humilitas* in describing William at all, but he incorporated humble avowals of unworthiness carried far beyond standard protestations. Despite changes in the concept of humility in the course of the twelfth century, humility was still regarded as one of the more important virtues, and contemporary ecclesiastics often gave it special emphasis. For example, the representation of the virtues on the central porch of Notre-Dame of Paris, done about 1210, portrayed

---

6. *Gesta*, p. 451: "Velut ancilla Christi, servilem se ostendebat personam et de facultatibus suis in persona propria, velut Christi pauper pauperibus ministrabat." Georges Duby, *Guerriers et paysans, VII–XIIe siècle: Premier essor de l'économie européenne* (Paris, 1973), p. 191.

7. *Gesta*, p. 452: "Tandem humilitatem ancille sue Dominus respeciens, tale de ejus sanctitate in vita sua exitu prestitit argumentum. . . . Paulum digressi breviter ista perstrinximus . . . ad honorem Dei, et instructionem nostram, quibus virtutem feminam Dominus proposuit in humilitatis et bonitatis exemplum."

humility as the chief of the virtues; and Bishop William of Bourges (1200–1209), a Cistercian abbot before his election, was described by his biographer as especially outstanding for his humility.[8] Though the biographer of William of Seignelay did not use the word humility in describing his subject, he found the virtue in William's mother and described acts indicating its presence in some form in William.

The biographer found other virtues to be necessary in a bishop besides those suitable in a saintly widow. He gave the most stress to wisdom. Like many twelfth-century hagiographers, he said that his subject matured early. William was never attracted to childhood games nor to the knightly discipline his father tried to teach him. Rather, he embraced the program of study his uncle set up for him when he entered the Sens cathedral school, advancing quickly through the liberal arts and civil and canon law to theology; he never attained the grade of *magister,* but he could have done so easily. The biographer further drew an explicit comparison between William's love of study and Solomon's love of Wisdom, "from which all good things come."[9]

Though the biographer described explicitly only William's sense of unworthiness and his love for wisdom, he went on to say that William was so shining with "virtue" that clerics and laymen could not help but love him. The local people, the biographer said, brought William all their problems, both temporal and spiritual; the bishop would sometimes stop to talk affectionately to them for so long that his party would grow impatient. As William died, according to the biographer, he manifested great love for the clerics around him. Sick with the same fever that had killed his beloved brother two years earlier, he spoke to those around him with "divine eloquence" and requested their prayers, urged the canons of Paris, where he was then bishop, to elect his successor promptly, and asked to be buried at Pontigny with his parents in front of the altar dedicated to St. Thomas Becket. He finally died "blessed in the Lord."[10] Since William was bishop of Paris when he died, while his biographer remained a canon at Auxerre, it

8. Adolf Katzenellenbogen, *Allegories of the Virtues and Vices in Medieval Art from Early Christian Times to the Thirteenth Century,* trans. Alan J. P. Crick (London, 1939), p. 75. *Vita S. Guilielmi archiepiscopi Bituricensis,* AASS Jan. 1:630.

9. *Gesta,* pp. 452–54: ". . . cum Salomone posset dicere, 'super salutem et omnem pulchritudinem dilexi sapientiam et proposui pro luce habere eam; venerunt mihi omnia bona pariter cum illa.' " This is perhaps paraphrased from 2 Para. 1.11–12. The topos of the *puer senex,* of the boy prematurely old in wisdom, was frequently used in the Middle Ages; it had roots both in the thought of late Antiquity and in the Bible. See Ernst Robert Curtius, *European Literature and the Latin Middle Ages,* trans. Willard R. Trask (New York, 1958), pp. 98–101.

10. *Gesta,* pp. 484–85.

is quite possible that this deathbed scene represents the biographer's notion of what a worthy bishop would say and do in his last days, rather than an actual report from the bedside. But it does indicate that, for the biographer, a bishop's close personal affection for those around him was essential, and William's demonstration of this affection was a sign of his holiness.

The biographer further compared William to his sainted cousin Bernard and his pious mother by describing his episcopate as attended by miracles. These miracles (unlike the miraculous averting of the storm when Hugh of Montaigu had withdrawn to Clairvaux) always accompanied William when he was involved in the pastoral or liturgical duties of his office. The first miracle to be described involved William's affection for local laymen. While two penitents were waiting to see him and be absolved, part of the roof of the episcopal palace collapsed, narrowly missing them—Hugh of Noyers had added a new cellar and a kitchen to the palace but done nothing to the roof. The biographer said that their escape was a manifest miracle and related that William called the multitude to praise God for this act of divine mercy, which held off death from the two until they were able to complete their penance. The biographer described similar miracles happening repeatedly when William began the construction of the new cathedral. A number of accidents took place as the old cathedral was demolished and the foundation for the new laid, and in every instance someone narrowly escaped death, which according to the biographer demonstrated that God gives a man a chance to repent of his sins before it is too late. Cathedral canons, workmen, and even some liturgical books were saved in various miracles. [11]

William built the cathedral for the glory of God, and God showed His approval by these miracles. The Romanesque church of Auxerre, in spite of the new windows Hugh of Noyers had let into the walls, was very dark, and its whole appearance, according to William's biographer, "suffered from squalor and old age." Many cathedrals of northern France were being rebuilt at the end of the twelfth century, usually because the old structures had come to be considered too small, too poor, or too somber. [12] The church of Auxerre must have suffered especially in comparison with the recently completed cathedral of Sens, also dedicated to St. Stephen, where William had spent many years of his life. Leaving only the Romanesque

11. Ibid., pp. 470–71, 475–79.
12. Augustin Fliche, Christine Touzellier, and Yvonne Azais, *La Chrétienté romaine (1198–1274)*, Histoire de l'église depuis les origines jusqu'à nos jours 10 (Paris, 1950), p. 411. *Gesta*, p. 474: "Videns itaque episcopus ecclesiam suam Autissiodorensem structure antique minusque composite squalore ac senio laborare. . . ."

crypt, William destroyed the old cathedral of Auxerre and began construction in the "new" Gothic style. Many pious gifts were made to help pay for the construction, but costs were borne especially by episcopal revenues earmarked for the purpose.[13] The biographer made the cathedral William's crowning achievement, a demonstration of his personal holiness and his excellence in office.

Defense of Episcopal Rights

William's excellence in office, according to his biographer, was also demonstrated in an administration that was "forceful" and thorough, due to the bishop's determination that nothing should happen "to the prejudice of his church." If the biographer saw any conflict between a bishop's personal deference and his administrative duty to pursue his own rights somewhat belligerently, he gave little indication of it. Contemporary charters and the biography itself indicate that William was sometimes involved in prolonged quarrels with other ecclesiastics, but the biographer regarded these quarrels as pious acts in defense of the church. He said that William followed the regulations for a bishop given by the Apostle and cited the verse from 1 Timothy 3.4, that a good bishop is one who "ruleth well his own house." William demonstrated this biblical attribute, the biographer said, by "pursuing his rights indefatigably," though the passage he cited immediately followed a verse proscribing litigiousness: a bishop should be "patient, not a brawler, not covetous."[14]

The biographer first showed William in indefatigable pursuit of his rights while still dean. He related in detail the quarrels between Bishop Hugh of Noyers and the chapter, led by William, over the judgment of ecclesiastical cases and the chapter's trees at Appoigny (see above, p. 107). The biographer described these instances as acts of self-defense on William's part, though from the evidence it seems that William was as much responsible as Hugh for beginning the first known quarrel between the bishop and the chapter of Auxerre in fifty years. Also as dean, according to the biographer, William obtained amends from the Premonstratensian canons of Notre-Dame-la-Dehors who had been ordained by the bishop without the presentation of the cathedral dean, a step which William considered necessary; he ordered the prior of Notre-Dame to do penance for several

---

13. *Gesta*, pp. 474–75. For an account of the construction during the thirteenth century, see Don Denny, "Some Narrative Subjects in the Portal Sculpture of Auxerre Cathedral," *Speculum* 51 (1976), 23–34.

14. *Gesta*, p. 461: ". . . juris sui infatigabilis prosequutor juxta regula Apostoli, 'Domui sue bene prepositus.' " Compare this with 1 Tim. 3.3–4: ". . . non litigiosum, non cupidum, sed suae domui bene praepositum."

days by eating only bread and water and not leaving the cloister because he had been "rebellious" and "inobedient." In addition, he said, William established that no cathedral canon should alienate property belonging to the chapter without the chapter's permission, under pain of excommunication.[15] Clearly the biographer's sympathies lay with William rather than with the episcopal office itself. Hugh of Noyers was simply one of many enemies against whom William had to defend his rights.

The biographer did, however, note with regret that, once William became bishop, he again made the bishop of Auxerre the first judge of ecclesiastical cases in the diocese, though as dean he had claimed this right for the dean. The biographer described this shift in policy as "oppression" of the dean, a sign of the "imperfection of human frailty,"[16] the only explicitly unfavorable remark he made about William. The biographer himself gave no details on this deplorable oppression, but a letter of Innocent III indicates that the quarrel between bishop and dean arose in 1208, shortly after William's consecration. William captured and imprisoned a priest accused of burglary. The dean demanded that William give the priest into his jurisdiction and pronounced interdict on the bishop's household until William should do so. William excommunicated the dean as incorrigible; the dean appealed to the pope; Innocent III pronounced William's excommunication of the dean proper but, unable to determine who should have jurisdiction over the burglar-priest, turned this question over to the bishop and chapter of Troyes. The final outcome of the case is unknown.[17] It is scarcely surprising that the biographer did not want to give the details of this unedifying quarrel, but the documents confirm the biographer's description of a bishop intent on preserving his rights. The case demonstrates the ease with which the pope could become involved in local affairs by the beginning of the thirteenth century, though the biographer did not mention this involvement.

The documents also indicate that William sometimes became embroiled in conflicts with the local churches in defense of his perceived rights. Like Hugh of Noyers, William came most frequently in conflict with St.-Germain, which as a house following Cluniac practices owed obedience to the abbot of Cluny as well as to the bishop of Auxerre. In 1216, William complained to Innocent III that the abbot of St.-Germain had impeded his procurator in making visits of correction to the abbey. When the pope ordered the abbot

15. Ibid., pp. 454–56.
16. Ibid., pp. 462–63: "Hoc in ipso precipuum repperimus de imperfecto fragilitatis humane."
17. Innocent III, Letter 10.189, PL 215:1288–89.

to remove all difficulties, the abbot of Cluny complained to Innocent that only he had the right of visitation over St.-Gemain. The quarrel was quite prolonged, but Innocent finally resolved it by declaring that Cluny should have the right of correction over matters concerning the order, that is, negligence with respect to the divine office or the monastic rule, while the bishop had correction in canonical cases, those involving criminal accusations and claims.[18] In another quarrel involving St.-Germain, the bishop and the abbot disagreed over the custom of *melicia* and its application in two of their *villae* which adjoined; it is unclear exactly what this *consuetudo* entailed, but it seems to have been rights over bee swarms.[19]

William also became involved in a dispute with the bishop of Autun over the Bethlehem chapel at Clamecy on the border of the two dioceses, a quarrel settled by mediators who included William's brother Manasses, bishop of Orléans. On another occasion, Manasses was among the mediators settling a quarrel between William and the abbess of St.-Julien over some houses the convent owned that infringed on episcopal water at the river's edge.[20]

Though the biographer found William's quarrel with his chapter an act of "oppression" and passed in complete silence over his quarrels with other ecclesiastics, he had nothing but praise for William's firm defense of his rights against the count. Like Hugh of Noyers, William had two counts to contend with, Peter, count of Auxerre, and Hervé, count of Nevers. While still dean, the biographer related, he had excommunicated Peter for injuries done to the property of the chapter, until Peter came to make amends.[21] As soon as he became bishop, William made it clear that he now considered himself the superior of the local secular rulers, both as their spiritual head and as their feudal lord. There had been for two centuries or more at Auxerre a custom that, on the day of a bishop's enthronement, the local nobility should carry him on their shoulders from St.-Germain to the cathedral.[22] When neither count appeared to perform this duty, William

18. Innocent III, Letter suppl. 216, PL 217:255. *Gallia Christiana* 12:153–54, no. 77.
19. Jean Lebeuf, *Mémoires concernant l'histoire civile et ecclésiastique d'Auxerre*, ed. and aug. Ambroise Challe and Maximilien Quantin, 4 (Auxerre, 1855), 86, no. 143. Bibl. Auxerre, Cart. St.-Germain, fol. 58v, no. 25. DuCange, *Glossarium mediae et infimae Latinitatis* 5:332, defines *melicia* as the drink mead, but this does not seem correct from the context. The charter edited hy Lebeuf is the only reference DuCange gives for a use of the word.
20. *Gallia Christiana* 12:148, 150–51, nos. 67, 72.
21. *Gesta*, p. 456.
22. This custom is first mentioned explicitly at the time of the consecration of Bishop Heribert in 1040 as an *aecclesiastica consuetudo*: ibid., p. 392. A similar custom was found at Paris, Bordeaux, and Soissons in the twelfth century. Imbart de la

demanded an explanation. Peter excused himself by saying that he had had to appear before the king that day and announced publicly that, as the bishop's man, he recognized his duty to carry all new bishops of Auxerre. Hervé, however, claimed that this duty devolved from the fief of Gien, which had now passed to the king; only after two years of intermittent quarreling did he agree that the duty of carrying a new bishop was hereditary, coming from his father and not attached to Gien.[23]

The counts' unwillingness to take part in a ceremony symbolizing their submission to the bishop was reflected in their refusal to recognize that they held certain of their castles in fief from him. The biographer spoke admiringly of how William finally persuaded the counts to do homage to him, "not without difficulty," and with "much labor and expense." Though Peter's predecessors had recognized that they held Mailly in fief from the bishop of Auxerre since the 1145 agreement between Count William II and Hugh of Mâcon, and had similarly done homage for Bétry since the 1157 agreement between William III and Bishop Alain, Peter declared that he held these castles in fief from the count of Champagne. In 1210, he even briefly persuaded the pope that the charters the bishop produced, attesting that Peter and his predecessors had held these castles from William's predecessors, were sealed with false seals. Count Hervé similarly refused to do homage for Cosne, St.-Sauveur, and Châteauneuf, all castles that the counts of Nevers had held in fief from the bishops of Auxerre since 1145. But William acted with such "prudence," according to his biographer, that he gained the submission of both counts. In 1211, after William persuaded the pope that the seals were not forged, Peter did homage for Mailly and Bétry, and, in 1215, as he was preparing to go to Constantinople, he added homage for Coulanges-sur-Yonne. The following year, his second wife Yolande declared herself to be the bishop's *femina* (the female equivalent of doing homage) for the three castles of Bétry, Mailly, and Coulanges-sur-Yonne, on behalf of her infant son Philip. Hervé finally agreed to do homage for Cosne, St.-Sauveur, and Châteauneuf in 1209, as he was leaving to fight the Albigensians, but only on the condition that William would not demand that Hervé give up Cosne at any time during his life.[24] The biographer did mention the assistance William re-

---

Tour, *Les élections épiscopales dans l'église de France du IXe au XIIe siècle* (Paris, 1891), p. 333; William Mendel Newman, *Les seigneurs de Nesle en Picardie (XIIe-XIIIe siècle)* (Paris and Philadelphia, 1971), 1:104.

23. *Gallia Christiana* 12:148-49, nos. 66, 68.

24. *Gesta*, pp. 471-74. Quantin 3.96, p. 43. *Gallia Christiana* 12:149-50, 153-54, nos. 69, 71, 76, 78.

ceived from the pope in these quarrels, though this was one of very few references in the biography to the papal curia. He gave quite a detailed account of William's triumph over the counts, as a record of the terms of the agreement and as a demonstration of the bishop's ability to defend his rights.

The biographer noted that William defended the rights of his chapter against the counts as vigorously as he defended his own. Around 1213, Hervé, back from southern France, built a fortress at Billy (37 kilometers southwest of Auxerre), adjacent to land belonging to the cathedral chapter; the chapter complained that their property was harmed by this fortress. William arranged a compromise, which his biographer called "very useful" to the church, by which the chapter gave Hervé their land at Billy in exchange for his property at Oisy, three kilometers away, where the chapter had had land since the time of Hugh of Montaigu. William also extracted homage for the new fortress from Hervé. In a similar case, the powerful lord Dreux of Mello erected gibbets outside his village of St.-Maurice-Thizouaille (sixteen kilometers west of Auxerre), which the chapter considered injurious to their adjoining property at Egleny. William intervened in favor of the chapter and persuaded Dreux to dismantle the gibbets. William's successful defense of his chapter's rights was, his biographer said, due to his "perseverance and strength" (*instantia et virtus*).[25]

The latter incident took place in 1219, when both bishop and chapter were finding it easier to defend their temporal possessions because the counts were no longer in Auxerre. In 1216, Peter had departed for Constantinople to claim the crown of the Latin empire after the removal of Emperor Henry, the brother of Peter's second wife Yolande. Before leaving, in order to raise money, he sold to the townspeople of Auxerre his castle and his right to levy fees of all sorts in the city, for an annual payment of 2000 pounds Provins; William was made responsible for collecting the money every year. In 1218, Hervé too took the cross and started for Egypt, but only after he had persuaded the pope that the bishops of Auxerre and Nevers should contribute to the upkeep of his companions on Crusade. Peter never returned to Auxerre but died in Turkish captivity, which Hugh of Noyers's biographer considered a warning against human pride.[26]

Hervé hurried home to Burgundy as soon as he heard rumors of Peter's death, intending to claim the county of Auxerre to add to his county of

25. *Gesta*, pp. 471–72. Quantin 3.216, p. 96. *Gallia Christiana* 12:152–53, no. 75. Arch. Yonne G 1846.
26. *Gesta*, p. 443. Lebeuf, *Histoire d'Auxerre* 4:80–82, 86, nos. 132, 142. Honorius III, Letter 2.1234, RHGF 19:661.

Nevers. He hesitated while William was still bishop and the rumors were still unconfirmed, but as soon as he learned that William was to be translated to Paris, he occupied the city by force and invited back men William had exiled from the city. The biographer described in horrified detail how they wrought heavy damage to church property, imprisoned many of the church's men, and even invaded the capitular chapter, wounding one canon with a sword and galloping over another. To the biographer, Hervé was a man of formidable cruelty who had only been restrained earlier because of William's forceful presence. The new bishop was unable to resist the count of Nevers. Hervé was unaffected by letters from the pope to the king and to Hervé, reminding the count that he was doing double offense to Christ in harming church property and in seizing the goods of one sealed with the cross—there was still some hope that Count Peter might be alive. Only Hervé's death brought relief to the churches of Auxerre. By comparing William's successful resistance to Hervé with the failure of his "kind and simple successor," the biographer made it clear that he expected a good administrator to be very firm with the local nobility. Few bishops could withstand a count such as Hervé as William had been able to do.[27]

William fought for his rights against the king with the same vigor with which he fought the local counts, though less successfully. His biographer gave the details of his first quarrel with Philip II immediately after the account of his election. The king, exercising the royal right of *spolatio*, had sent his men to seize the temporal regalia of the bishopric as soon as Hugh of Noyers died. This is the first instance at Auxerre for which full details survive on this royal right. Count William II had renounced any such comital rights at the beginning of Humbaud's pontificate, and Louis VI and Louis VII had not exercised the royal right of *spolatio* at Auxerre, though they did at other sees. Philip II had seized the temporal regalia of Auxerre while the canons were quarreling over the election of Hugh of Noyers, but no details survive of this action other than a brief mention by Robert of St.-Marien.[28]

When the see of Auxerre fell vacant in 1206, Philip again seized the regalia. William's biographer said that he was plundering the bishop's property in the guise of protecting it. The biographer and Robert of St.-Marien give similar accounts of William's prompt response to this plundering.[29]

27. *Gesta*, pp. 482–83: ". . . successorem ipsius Henricum magne quidem benignitatis et simplicitatis virum, atrocius infestavit." Honorius III, Letter 4.823, RHGF 19:704.
28. Jean-François Lemarignier, Jean Gaudemet, and Guillaume Mollat, *Institutions ecclésiastiques*, Histoire des institutions françaises au moyen âge 3 (Paris, 1962), p. 246. Robert of St.-Marien, p. 244.
29. *Gesta*, pp. 460–61. Robert of St.-Marien, p. 271.

Immediately after his election, he demanded the regalia, but Philip would not release them until William had been confirmed and consecrated by the archbishop. This does not seem to have been an unusual demand, for it was the French practice that the king only invested a new bishop with the regalia after he was consecrated, and popes and decretists agreed that a bishop could not begin to administer church property until he was confirmed.[30] But the delay meant that many trees had been cut in episcopal forests and many moveable goods carried away from episcopal houses by the time William received the regalia; he demanded payment to compensate for the losses. After a good deal of effort and several well-placed bribes, according to his biographer, he received not only the compensation but also a royal privilege that, whenever the see should be vacant in the future, the chapter rather than the king would administer the regalia. The biographer considered the attainment of this privilege as one of the great successes of William's episcopacy and mentioned it again later when summing up William's improvements to the bishopric.[31]

The king however had granted this privilege with the stipulation that the bishop would continue to owe him knights and forty days of personal army duty; a few years later, this royal claim became the basis of a prolonged quarrel between King Philip on the one hand and William and his brother Manasses on the other. The biographer could scarcely ignore a quarrel that lasted nearly two years and drove the bishops of both Auxerre and Orléans into exile, but he minimized its significance by describing it in his section on Manasses's pontificate at Orléans, barely mentioning, at the end of his description, that the quarrel involved William as well as his brother. A number of papal and royal documents fill in the details.[32]

By the end of the twelfth century, decretists had agreed that bishops with regalia owed the king the service of a certain number of knights and were even required to accompany the king's army in person, though not to fight themselves.[33] In 1210, King Philip came to Auxerre in William's absence and ordered some of the bishop's knights to join his army, which they refused to do. Declaring that William and Manasses had failed to provide their required knights, Philip proceeded to seize the temporal regalia

30. Robert L. Benson, *The Bishop-Elect* (Princeton, 1968), pp. 115, 366-67.
31. *Gesta*, p. 480.
32. Ibid., pp. 464-66. Innocent III, Letters 14.52, 15.39-40, 108-09, PL 216:417-21, 570-74, 619-20. Quantin 3.116, p. 53. Lebeuf, *Histoire d'Auxerre* 4:72, no. 113.
33. Robert L. Benson, "The Obligations of Bishops with 'Regalia.' Canonistic Views from Gratian to the Early Thirteenth Century," *Proceedings of the Second International Congress of Medieval Canon Law*, ed. Stephan Kuttner and J. Joseph Ryan (Vatican City, 1965), pp. 128-30.

in retaliation, in spite of his renunciation of any right to the regalia of Auxerre just a few years earlier. Both bishops were then afraid to return to their sees and complained to Innocent III that they had been driven into exile.

Innocent, whose mediating role William's biographer did not mention, first assigned the case to the arbitration of the archbishop of Sens. The archbishop, unable to make the two sides agree, laid an interdict on Philip's lands (May–June, 1212), and the pope finally had to mediate the case himself. Philip said the bishops had not been exiled but were free to return whenever they liked, and that he had had every right to seize the regalia, since their sees were as good as empty now that they had failed to perform their required army duty. The bishops complained in turn that the king had seized not only the temporal regalia of their sees but also tithes and prebends, to which he was never entitled.[34] They also said that they were not at fault since they had had no idea that their knights had refused to follow the king.

Philip promised the pope he would make concessions if the interdict were lifted, but the concessions he made were few. The bishops regained the regalia and were freed from personal army duty during their lifetimes, but the king made no amends for the damages he had done to episcopal property, and the bishops agreed to bring no suit concerning the damages. The king also made the bishops promise that they would bring no case of canonical irregularity against any of Philip's men and women who had married during the interdict, though normally all marriages performed during an interdict were considered illicit. The king had become too powerful for the bishop of Auxerre to oppose on his own, and even with the pope's assistance, the bishop had to make more concessions to the king than the king made to him. William's biographer described William and Manasses as overcoming the king with "long-suffering," "great labor," "constancy," and "strength." By the beginning of the thirteenth century such attributes were insufficient for success against the king of France.

The biographer presented William as the strong defender of his church and its rights, even though other evidence suggests that William's successes in this area were somewhat qualified. His major triumphs were in making improvements to the churches of Auxerre; the construction of the new

---

34. The king had recently begun claiming the spiritual as well as temporal regalia during a vacancy, a practice of which most ecclesiastics disapproved. Jean Gaudemet, *Collation par le roi des bénéfices vacants en régale des origines à la fin du XIVe siècle* (Paris, 1935), p. 3. John W. Baldwin, *Masters, Princes and Merchants: The Social Views of Peter the Chanter and His Circle* (Princeton, 1970), 1:250.

cathedral was his great achievement. But the biographer opened his account of William's activities as bishop with an account of his new foundations and liturgical innovations.

Administration as Innovation

The biographer began his description of the characteristics William showed as bishop by saying that his "administration was forceful and thorough," that he allowed nothing to be done unless he himself had first given it "full deliberation."[35] He showed William as chiefly giving his deliberation to the "amplification of the divine cult"—he founded several new churches in the diocese, the first new foundations for half a century. The biographer gave William the credit for establishing a collegiate chapter of canons at Toucy and a chapter of the Hospitallers of Montjou at Appoigny, though the documents indicate that both of these chapters had been founded during the pontificate of Hugh of Noyers, without his assistance or confirmation, and that William simply confirmed the foundations and issued detailed regulations governing their canonical life. The biographer also mentioned the foundation of a collegiate chapter in the episcopal city of Cosne, and he credited William with the establishing of Cistercian nuns at Celles (three kilometers west of Auxerre), Carthusians at Beaulieu, and the brothers of the order of Val-des-Choux at Epeau, near Donzy (Val-des-Choux had been founded in 1193 on a combination of Cistercian and Carthusian principles). William's surviving documents fill in the details on these monastic or collegiate foundations, but the biographer made at least passing mention of all of them.[36] Information on the new parish churches William established is given only in his documents. William made the chapel at the castle of Bétry into a parish church; Bétry, 20 kilometers southeast of Auxerre, was held in fief from the bishop by the counts, and William considered it too far from the nearest church for easy access to the sacraments. At La Charité, where the heresy that Hugh had tried to exterminate had emerged again, William established two more parishes in a

---

35. *Gesta*, p. 461: "In administratione suscepta strenuus fuit valde et providus, etpote qui nichil agebat ex precipti, nec quicquam quod se suis sollicitudinibus ingeret faciendum, prodire sinebat in actum, nisi prius multa fuisset deliberationis fornace decoctum."

36. Ibid., pp. 471-72. For the chapter at Toucy, see Lebeuf, *Histoire d'Auxerre* 4:71-72, no. 111; 74-75, no. 117. For the Hospitallers, ibid., pp. 83-84, nos. 137-38. For the nuns of Celles, see *Gallia Christiana* 12:154-55, nos. 79-80. For the chapter at Cosne, see Lebeuf, *Histoire d'Auxerre* 4:73, no. 115.

town that had had only one, hoping that increased pastoral care would help reduce the threat of heresy.[37]

William's new foundations were thus intended to improve the religious life of his diocese, by establishing some houses for the spiritual benefit of men and women who wished to take orders, by giving other houses detailed regulations to insure the regularity of their life, and by creating new parish churches for the advantage of the laymen of the diocese. The number of parish churches increased throughout western Europe at the beginning of the thirteenth century. Although some ecclesiastics, such as the moral theologian Peter the Chanter, spoke out strongly against any multiplication of parishes, fearing this would increase litigation without improving the care of souls, new parishes were generally seen as necessary in the cities to serve the increasing population and in the country to give people less far to travel to church.[38]

William also attempted to improve the diocese's religious life by elaboration of the cathedral's liturgical observance. While still dean of the chapter, the biographer recorded, William added the Office of the Virgin to the celebration of the canonical hours on feast days, replaced the simple "Alleluia" of the hours with antiphons of the Psalms, and made several other changes in the liturgy, "adding what was good" or "subtracting what was bad."[39] As bishop, the biographer continued, William separated the feasts of Sts. Alexander and Bris, which had been celebrated together "due to some confusion" (St. Bris was a third-century martyr of the Auxerrois); made the feast of the Apostles a solemn festival, accompanied by decoration of the church, ringing of the great bells, and lighting of extra candles; and established a new ceremony for the cathedral canons on the eve of the feast of St. Stephen, the cathedral's patron.[40]

For the better celebration of the Mass, the biographer said that William established new prebends for the lector and succentor. These two officers had previously shared a single prebend with the magister, and since the revenues of the prebend were very scanty when divided three ways, no one had wished to undertake any of the offices. Now, with the consent of his whole chapter, William set up prebends adequate for the lector and succentor. In addition, the biographer related that William and his sacristan estab-

---

37. Lebeuf, *Histoire d'Auxerre* 4:75, no. 118. Innocent III, Letter 13.211, PL 216: 376–78.

38. Baldwin, *Masters, Princes, and Merchants* 1:70. Lemarignier, Gaudemet, and Mollat, *Institutions ecclésiastiques*, p. 198.

39. *Gesta*, p. 456: "Multaque alia ad honestatem divionorum consensu capituli vel adjecit, vel exterminavit penitus, vel mutavit."

40. Ibid., p. 469.

lished several new caretakers in the church (*matricularii*), some clerics and some laymen, to ring the bells, make sure that all that was necessary for the Mass was on hand, and keep the church clean.[41]

All these details were, for the biographer, practical achievements worth recording for posterity, new and better ways of promoting the religious life of Auxerre. In stressing William's successful innovation, he did not give details on the more ordinary administrative business of a bishop: witnessing pious gifts to the local houses or settling ecclesiastical disputes. The documents, however, indicate that William was very concerned for the well-being of all diocesan churches, both old and new, in spite of his own occasional quarrels with these churches. He was frequently among the witnesses when a layman made a gift to a local monastery, much more often than had been the case with Hugh of Noyers (an average of 1.9 versus 0.4 such existing charters a year). When a laymen drew up a charter attesting to the end of his quarrel with a religious house, William was again often among the witnesses and might even be asked to excommunicate the layman if he tried to go back on his word, as a guarantee of the firmness of the agreement.[42] In 1219, he settled a long-standing quarrel between St.-Germain, a house with which he himself had quarreled, and one Renaud of Diges, who held some land in fief from the abbey and had apparently made this tenure a pretext to seize other property of the abbey and harass the monks and the other tenants. William forced Renaud to swear on the Bible that he would give up all violence. Examples from Pontigny, Crisenon, St.-Marien, Reigny, and Notre-Dame-la-Cité could be added.[43] The fact that William was so frequently called on to settle differences involving the local churches indicates that his arbitration was considered a guarantee that a settlement would be observed. His reputation as a peacemaker was such that he was sometimes designated by the pope as arbiter of quarrels outside his diocese, as was the case in 1216 when he settled the dispute between a certain cleric and the abbey of St.-Mauré-des-Fossés, near Paris.[44]

The documents indicate that the pope was a frequent presence in William's diocesan administration. He often confirmed William's adminis-

41. Ibid., pp. 468–69. *Gallia Christiana* 12:151–52, no. 74. Lebeuf, *Histoire d'Auxerre* 4:77, no. 124.

42. As in the 1213 quarrel between the count and the abbey of Reigny: Quantin 3.135, p. 62.

43. For St.-Germain, ibid., 3.226, pp. 99–100. For Pontigny, ibid., 3.80, p. 40. For Crisenon, ibid., 3.167, pp. 76–77. For St.-Marien, see Arch. Yonne H 1276. For Reigny, see Arch. Yonne H 1640, no. 900. For Notre–Dame, see Lebeuf, *Histoire d'Auxerre* 4:73, no. 116.

44. Arch. Nat. S 1181B, no. 23.

trative acts, even his establishment of *matricularii* in the cathedral, although such an arrangement might seem to have a purely local purpose. But most frequently William and the pope corresponded on the subject of heresy. The biographer, who barely mentioned the pope's role in diocesan affairs, made no allusion to the dangers to orthodoxy from heretics, usurers, and Jews, but these concerns are frequent in William's letters. The Cathars at La Charité remained the chief threat to orthodoxy in the diocese, especially the heresiarchs who called themselves *consolatores*, but the usurers who congregated there were considered nearly as dangerous. Innocent therefore granted William the right to proceed against all these heretics without the fear that his decisions might be appealed, for the purpose of better keeping the "wolves from the sheepfold" and the "tares from the field." The pope also approved William's decision to make the Jews of the Auxerrois pay the ecclesiastical tithes due from any lands or vineyards they purchased; though at the time of Hugh of Noyers at least some of the Jews had been driven from the diocese, there were apparently still a number there.[45]

The biographer also failed to indicate that William was present at the ecumenical council Lateran IV, which the pope held in 1215; a contemporary list of participants includes William. This council prohibited the formation of new religious orders, declared yearly communion necessary for all Christians, and, most importantly, emphasized the refutation of heresies and formulated a new statement of the Christian faith, more elaborate than the creeds of Nicea or Constantinople.[46] But the biographer does not seem to have considered it important to show his subject as an integral part of the wider church, for he made no mention of William's defense of orthodoxy or his participation in decisions affecting the religious life of all Christians.

He does seem to have considered it appropriate to show William as an innovator, one who replaced the old or worn out with the new and improved. He recorded that William gave his church several ornamental hangings, added a new roof and new windows to the episcopal palace, obtained liege homage for some land in the city of Auxerre and in Varzy which several nobles had held, removed the tithes of Sancerre from the hands of the count of Sancerre, and obtained the entire jurisdiction over the village of Charbuy. In addition, he said that the bishop made many

---

45. Innocent III, Letters 10.204, 206, 61, PL 215: 1308-09, 1213-13, 1157-58.
46. Raymonde Foreville, *Latran I, II, III et Latran IV* (Paris, 1965), pp. 275-86, 392. Hefele-Leclercq, *Histoire des conciles*, 5, 2:1316-98.

other new acquisitions but that he could not remember them all.[47] This innovative aspect is seen throughout his account of William's administration, but especially in the decision to build a new cathedral.

It is indicative of the value the biographer placed on William's administrative abilities that, immediately after describing this new cathedral's construction, he gave an account of Pope Honorius III's judgment that William would make the best bishop of Paris. Honorius said in his own letters that, due to William's "excellent reputation and virtues," he would make a much more suitable bishop of Paris than any of the candidates proposed by different factions of the Paris chapter. The protests of both William and the Paris chapter proved in vain—William was even threatened with excommunication if he did not accept his new see—and in 1220 Willam left Auxerre for Paris, where he spent the remaining three years of his life bringing order to the local churches and defending episcopal prerogatives, much as he had done at Auxerre. In this case, the pope and William's biographer evidently agreed on what characteristics made a man a worthy bishop.[48]

The biographer said that, as bishop of Paris, William defended episcopal prerogatives against the king and pacified the tumultuous student quarter. He added that William did "many other outstanding things" in Paris, "worthy of being remembered forever," but that he would not detail them because the long list would induce boredom (*fastidium*) in the reader and because he did not know all the details himself. The scantiness of his knowledge did not keep him from feeling assured that whatever William had done, it had been praiseworthy, and that he had brought a "tranquil conclusion" to all affairs.[49]

Conclusions

The biographer described a man who in his view exemplified all the best traits of a bishop: William defended his rights and property, made many acquisitions and liturgical innovations, and built a new cathedral. His attributes were approved by the pope, who decided to translate him to Paris, and by God. The biographer's admiration for William is highlighted by the contrast he drew between William's episcopacy and his brother Manasses's episcopacy at Orléans. The biographer first distinguished the two bishops by saying that even as a boy William had been quicker at his

47. *Gesta*, pp. 472-73.
48. Ibid., pp. 479-82. Honorius III, Letter 4.783, RHGF 19:698-99. Second Continuator of Robert of St.-Marien, p. 286.
49. *Gesta*, pp. 484-85.

letters than his older brother, and Manasses had had to learn maturity from his younger brother. The biographer related William's successes against the count in detail; he described the two bishops' prolonged and unsatisfactory struggle with the king only in the section on Manasses. He described William's construction of a new cathedral at length, only briefly mentioning his other improvements to episcopal property; he recorded that Manasses built a new and expensive episcopal palace. William always ended his local disputes amicably; Manasses once provoked an armed rebellion in trying to enforce the payment of tithes. The biographer found nothing objectionable in itself in a new palace or quarrels with laymen, but his comparisons between Manasses and William were designed to praise William, the good bishop who spent his money on a cathedral, not a palace, and ended all his quarrels peacefully and victoriously.[50]

The biographer described this successful bishop as the only authority in the diocese. Although other sources tend to confirm his view that William was a very effective administrator, they make it clear that, at the beginning of the thirteenth century, the bishop of Auxerre was no longer the sole authority in local ecclesiastical affairs. The large jump in the amount of episcopal business at the beginning of the thirteenth century—William left over five times as many documents for each year of his episcopacy as did Hugh of Noyers—was in many ways a response to the growing amount of business at the royal and papal curiae, much of it concerned with local diocesan affairs. Philip II left over three times as many surviving charters as Louis VII, in a reign a few months shorter, and Innocent II left an average of 280 letters for each year of his pontificate, compared to 179 for Alexander III, the last outstanding lawyer-pope to precede him.[51] New trends were affecting the churches of France: the urge to build new cathedrals which the biographer welcomed; the growing legalism which swelled the church archives; and also the increasingly frequent presence of king and pope in the temporal and spiritual affairs of local dioceses.

50. Ibid., pp. 463–68.
51. Robert Fawtier, *The Capetian Kings of France: Monarchy and Nation*, trans. Lionel Butler and R. J. Adam (London, 1960), p. 8. R. W. Southern, *Western Society and the Church in the Middle Ages* (Harmondsworth, Eng., 1970), p. 109.

CONCLUSIONS

The duties of office required a bishop of Auxerre to show administrative ability. The biographers of the bishops also expected their subjects to demonstrate some type of spirituality: holiness of life, concern for the hereafter, and an orientation toward God. Over the course of the twelfth century, however, there were progressive changes in the definition both of spirituality and of proper administration. There were likewise changes in the way the bishops responded to the demands made on them in both spheres.

Since both the bishops and their biographers often equated the spiritual life with a withdrawn and contemplative search for holiness, whereas administration meant taking an active and vigorous part in worldly affairs, spirituality and administrative ability were to some extent incompatible episcopal attributes. Throughout much of the century, the biographers alternated in whether they laid the most stress on personal spirituality or on administrative achievements. This alternation reflects at least in part the desires of the canons, who tended to choose each time a bishop who displayed the attributes his predecessor had lacked. In part it reflects the rhetorical needs of the biographer, who, writing during the episcopate of his subject's successor, tended to stress those attributes that the present bishop did not seem to have.

Humbaud, who became bishop just as the reforms of the late eleventh century were beginning to have a significant impact at the local level, spent much of his episcopate restoring order in the chaotic affairs of his diocese. His successor, the monk Hugh of Montaigu, instead spent many of his years as bishop in the seclusion of the cloister; according to his biographer, he was "not very assiduous" in seeing to those affairs Humbaud had left unfinished. Hugh of Montaigu was in turn succeeded by Hugh of Mâcon, who proved very effective in handling the increasingly complex details of diocesan administration, rejecting "too much humility," in his biographer's words, in favor of a firm stand against local laymen. His successor Alain was again a monk who preferred the cloister; faced with the increased administrative demands of the episcopal office, he resigned to return to "fasts, prayers, and readings" performed in solitude. The episcopate of his successor, William of Toucy, was again marked by a profusion of administrative activity; his biographer called him "humble" but primarily used the term to describe his interest in the performance of the liturgy and the welfare of the local houses. The succeeding bishop, Hugh of Noyers, was another active administrator, but he suffered in comparison with William, in the eyes of his two biographers, because of his great display of wealth, his oppression of other ecclesiastics, and his misdirection of church funds. Finally, William of Seignelay was described in almost hagiographical terms by a biographer who stressed his family relations with saints and the miracles that attended his construction of a new cathedral. But the biographer also noted William's administrative success in resisting the count's depredations and in founding new churches. More than any of his twelfth-century predecessors, William managed to reconcile within himself the conflicting aspects of the bishop's role.

Superimposed on this alternation in the relative importance the biographers of Auxerre gave to episcopal spirituality and administrative ability are changes in the definition of these attributes and in the part they were expected to play in the bishop's fulfillment of his duties. Over the course of the twelfth century spirituality clearly experienced a relative decline in importance among the qualities desired in a bishop. For the episcopates of Humbaud to William of Toucy, a period in which the bishops alternated in displaying a predominantly spiritual orientation or devoting themselves chiefly to administrative affairs, the overall shift in the expectations concerning a bishop's attributes can be seen in whether these bishops' outstanding attributes were considered appropriate or not. The change is especially evident in the meaning assigned to "humility." Monastic poverty and humility were, according to Hugh of Montaigu's biographer, the chief sign of the bishop's blessedness and his fitness for office. But Hugh of Mâcon's biographer saw "too much" humility as an impediment to good administration, Alain's humility was an impetus to resign, William of Toucy's biographer redefined humility to be virtually synonymous with diocesan administration, and Hugh of Noyers's official biographer approvingly called his subject not humble but "magnificent."

With respect to administration, Humbaud and his vigorous reform of the diocese stand somewhat outside the general trend. His immediate successor, Hugh of Montaigu, had an episcopate in which administration was less emphasized than in any other; his biographer mentioned his new monastic foundations but did not discuss his temporal administration at all, a topic on which the documents, too, are silent. But administrative ability became increasingly important for his successors. Hugh of Mâcon's biographer made pointed comparisons between Hugh of Montaigu and Hugh of Mâcon, in favor of the latter's greater concern for temporal administration. Alain, whose administration, both diocesan and temporal, consisted of little more than reconfirmations of what his predecessors had done, was criticized for this by his contemporaries and seems to have felt his inadequacies sharply himself. William of Toucy's biographer described his bishop's administrative ability as encompassing all his activities and decisions. Hugh of Noyers's biographer thought his subject worthy primarily for his ability in temporal administration and considered his greatest failing a lack of sufficient attention to diocesan administration. Even in the case of William of Seignelay, whose biographer dwelt on his personal virtues in an attempt to make him a synthesis of all ideal episcopal qualities, it was clear that he would not have met the episcopal ideal without real ability and interest in diocesan and temporal administration, with which no excess of humility could be allowed to interfere.

The relative decline in the emphasis put on spirituality in these biographies need not be considered an indication that the biographers no longer thought it important that their subjects be virtuous. Rather, it is a reflection of what Vauchez has called the increasing variety of religious life in the twelfth century. At the beginning of the century, there was little doubt among ecclesiastics that the monk was closest to God of all men, but over the course of the century there was an increased conception of the possibility of multiple paths to salvation, even including ones for laymen living in the world.[1] The manifestation of inward spiritual life that the biographers of the late twelfth and early thirteenth centuries found most appropriate in a bishop was immersion in the administrative duties of the office. Thus William of Seignelay's biographer pictured his subject as someone whose saintliness was manifested in a defense of ecclesiastical rights and close attention to the affairs of his church. Spirituality and administration were for him essentially one.

Certainly there was a growing need throughout the twelfth century for bishops with solid administrative ability—which generally precluded a strong monastic vocation—because of the great increase in the amount and complexity of episcopal business during the course of the century. Bishops' chanceries generated more and more charters as bishops involved themselves in the affairs of all the churches of the diocese and arrived at increasingly legalistic solutions. Bishops also reacted to the growing role

1. André Vauchez, *La spiritualité du moyen âge occidental, VIIIe-XIIe siècles* (Paris, 1975), pp. 6, 168-70.

played by outside authorities, the king and the pope, in local ecclesiastical affairs. The pope's presence especially encouraged greater systematization in local church administration; ecumenical councils decreed uniform procedures for all bishops, whose decisions might well be appealed to Rome. Thus the canons of French cathedrals found it increasingly desirable to elect men with a strong orientation toward administration, which in practice usually meant former officers of the cathedral chapter.[2]

But the multiplication of ways to salvation meant that, if the biographers at Auxerre were equating episcopal spirituality with thorough and just administration, other ecclesiastics were seeking holiness through a rejection of the world's affairs much more radical than that embraced by the monastic bishops of the early twelfth century. The Franciscan Order, founded during the episcopate of William of Seignelay, quickly drew hordes of adherents attracted by the sanctity and closeness to Christ promised in its life of humility and poverty;[3] at the same time, however, William's biographer was able to describe his subject as virtuous without having him adopt either attribute. Episcopal spirituality, in becoming identified with administrative ability, grew to be one of a large number of recognized ways to salvation, but a way separate from that of the religious enthusiasts. From the close of the twelfth century onward, the church turned increasingly to the secular clergy for her bishops and elsewhere for her saints.

---

2. Constance B. Bouchard, "The Geographical, Social, and Ecclesiastical Origins of the Bishops of Auxerre and Sens in the Central Middle Ages," *Church History* 46 (1977), 287–90.
3. See Michel Mollat, "Pauvres et pauvreté a la fin du XIIe siècle," *Revue d'ascétique et de mystique* 41 (1965), 322–24.